THE ENGLISH GRAMMAR WORKBOOK FOR ADULTS

The English Grammar Workbook for Adults

A Self-Study Guide to Improve Functional Writing

Michael DiGiacomo

CALLISTO PUBLISHING

Copyright © 2020 by Callisto Publishing LLC
Cover and internal design © 2020 by Callisto Publishing LLC
Art Director: Rachel Haeseker
Art Producer: Tom Hood
Editor: Natasha Yglesias

Callisto Publishing and the colophon are registered trademarks of Callisto Publishing LLC.

Published by Callisto Publishing LLC C/O Sourcebooks LLC
P.O. Box 4410, Naperville, Illinois 60567-4410
(630) 961-3900
callistopublishing.com

Printed and bound in China.
WKT 23

CONTENTS

INTRODUCTION

Hey, everyone! Thanks for picking up this book. I'm a native New Yorker who started on an English teaching journey in 1994 in Sendai, Japan. At first, I thought teaching English would be easy. Boy, was I surprised! Sure, English has a lot of grammar rules, but I soon realized that in many situations, those rules, their exceptions, and even some "non-rules" made learning and teaching English pretty tough. For example, I knew that in English, we use *many* before countable nouns (*many pens, many people*) and *much* before uncountable nouns (*much rain, much love*). But one day, one of my students said, "I ate much food last night," which sounded weird to me. When I tried to figure out why, I couldn't find the answer in any of the grammar books I had. I realized that while most books will teach you how to make the grammar (the structure), they don't teach you how to apply it. That's how I became motivated to write this book. The lessons here will help you become more articulate and confident using English in your writing and everyday English conversations.

What Does This Book Mean by "Functional" English Grammar?

When something is functional, it's both practical and useful. The cat or dog on your coffee mug looks nice, but it's neither practical nor useful. Your mug will work just as well without the graphics. I wanted to write a book that would help clear up questions you may have about grammar but also give you opportunities to practice using grammar in real everyday situations. Applying what you learn is key to remembering and mastering anything. You have to *just do it*, as a certain sportswear company says. You can read all about swimming and spend hours watching swimming videos on YouTube, but to become a swimmer, you have to actually jump in the pool. So, welcome to your new "swimming area"!

So, what actually is grammar? The Merriam-Webster dictionary defines grammar as "the study of the classes of words, their inflections, and their functions and relations in the sentence." This definition really describes everything you need to know about grammar in order to write and speak English with proficiency. The classes of words are the parts of speech—nouns, adjectives, prepositions, conjunctions, pronouns, etc. Inflections refer to the way we use words to account for tense (past, present, future), mood, gender, voice, etc. And functions and relations are how words work together in a sentence.

There's a saying that you don't need to know how a clock works in order to tell time. The same goes for grammar. The different sections of this book are categorized by name so they can be presented in an organized way, but don't get caught up in the terminology. You don't need to remember the term *countable noun*—you just need to know that some nouns are countable, like dogs or cars, and that uncountable nouns refer to nouns that cannot be counted, like air. Learn the rules, practice with the exercises provided here, and keep this book on hand for easy reference!

How to Use This Book

This book is divided into two parts. The first part is a collection of the most practical and commonly used English grammar patterns. Each section is designed to give you a concise review of that grammar pattern, including its structure, meaning, and, most importantly, usage. At the end of each lesson, you'll find an exercise to give you some practice. You can check your answers with the answer key at the back of the book.

Once you feel comfortable with the grammar lessons, you can move on to part two. There, you'll find real-world scenarios in which you can apply what you learned in part one. These scenarios cover everything from social situations, school, and work life to creative writing.

This book is not a complete guide to English grammar. There are lots of those kinds of books on the market. Instead, this book focuses on the parts of English grammar that are most used in the real world. Recommendations for further reading can be found in the resources section at the end of this book.

A Note to Instructors

Thanks for selecting this book for your students. These lessons will be useful for any student who's learning to apply written grammar in a communicative way. The emphasis here is on practical usage. If you're teaching ESL/EFL, this book can help high-level English learners clear up any grammar points they may find fuzzy or confusing. Many of these lessons were born from the questions of my upper-level English learners. If you're working with native-level learners, you can use these lessons to help your students fill in any gaps they may have in their written English. Students can use this book as a self-study tool, a supplement to the material they're learning in class, or even an inspiration for out-of-class assignments.

A Note to ESL/EFL Students

In the twenty-five-plus years that I've been helping English learners like you, I've gotten more questions about grammar than any other area of English. It seems that even though ESL/EFL students take lots of grammar classes, those lessons can be confusing. Look at these two sentences:

If I win the lottery, I will buy a house.
If I won the lottery, I would buy a house.

The grammar is correct in both cases, but how about the real-world usage? In what situations do we use *if* followed by a present verb (*win*) or *if* followed by a past verb (*won*)? This book will help you set things straight as you learn how and when we use certain grammar patterns. This is a guidebook for your journey across the bridge from learning English to confidently using English in all the different areas of your life. It's your road map out of the fog and into the sunshine. So, put on your sunglasses, and let's get the proverbial ball rolling!

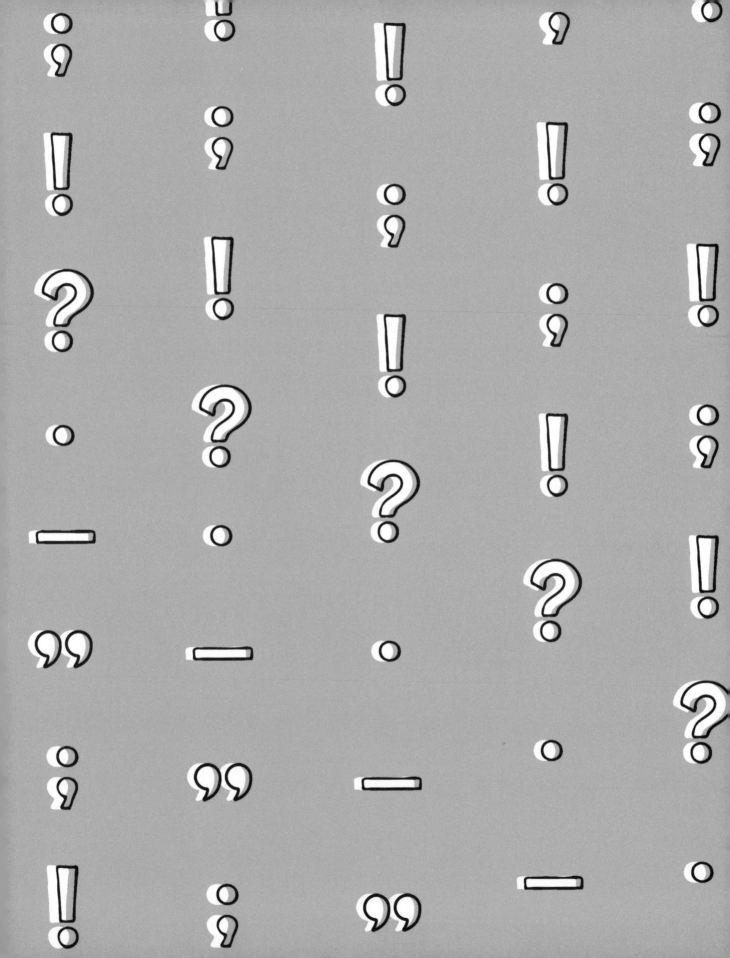

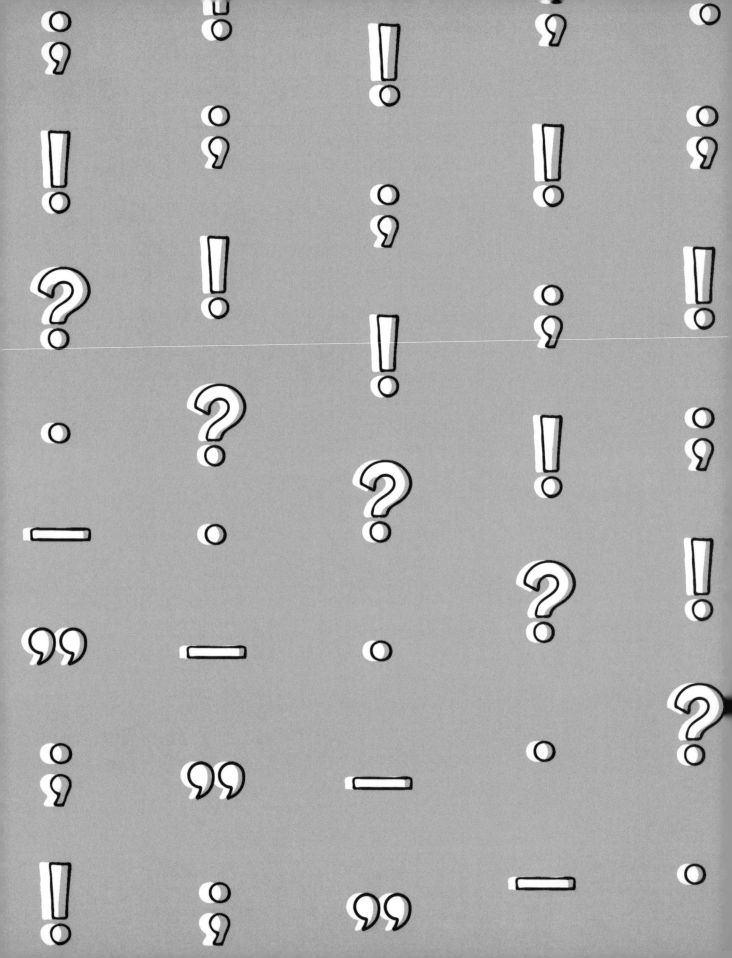

PART ONE

BY THE BOOK

In this part, we'll look at the most essential elements of American English grammar. If you often find yourself confused about how to use words like *a* and *the* or if you aren't sure if you should say "more happy" or "happier," this section will help. Topics are presented in a logical order, starting with words and then moving to sentences and finally paragraphs. Each topic is self-contained, so you can start anywhere and skip parts you're already confident with.

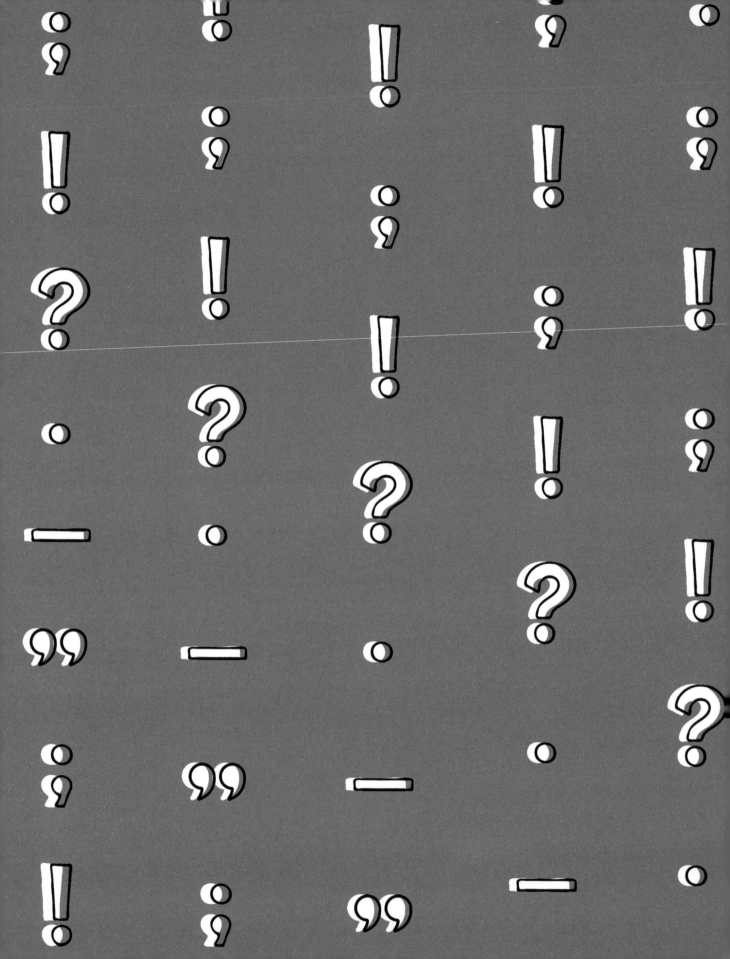

Chapter One

Nouns, Determiners, and Quantifiers

Have you ever played "20 Questions"? The first question is usually "Is it an animal, vegetable, or mineral?" Nouns, all of them. We'll explore the different types of nouns and learn about the determiners and quantifiers that support them.

Nouns

A **noun** is a word that represents a person, place, or thing. **Proper nouns**, always capitalized, name a specific person or thing, like *Maria* or *Paris*. **Common nouns** represent things in general, like *girl* or *city*. Many of these nouns represent things we can count, like *pens* and *people*. Some nouns represent things that we can't count, like *water* and *air*. Knowing this is important because these two types of nouns affect your grammar choices. For example, you can say "a pen," but you can't say "a water" or "a fun." We'll look at all the various types of nouns.

Countable Nouns

In general, **countable nouns** represent things that are concrete and tangible. Countable nouns are words that stand for people, places, or things that we can look at and count when there are more than one. Take a look around you. Maybe there are two or three pens, a few books, and some chairs. In your house, you may have two or more people living with you. Your town may have multiple shops, parks, and movie theaters. All of these types of words—pens, books, chairs, people, shops, parks, and theaters—are countable.

There are usually two forms for every countable noun. The *singular noun* is the form that shows one single thing, like *pen, dog,* and *park*. The *plural noun* is the noun that shows more than one thing, like *pens, dogs,* and *parks*.

Here are examples of countable nouns:

1. There is one *notebook* on the desk, and there are two *books* on the shelf.
2. Rohan has 12 *students* in his writing class.
3. What do you think of when you see all of those *stars*?

Exercise 1
Now it's your turn to practice.

---

1. Write about where you live. Are there many stores, museums, or restaurants in your town? How many parks are there?
2. Write about your kitchen. How many glasses do you have? Do you have any fruit, like apples or bananas? Does your kitchen have a lot of appliances?

Special Plural Nouns

In many cases, adding an **-s** or **-es** at the end of the word forms the plural spelling of nouns; however, there are a number of special spelling rules in English. These rules often depend on the vowels or consonants that the noun ends in.

1. When the noun ends in a vowel followed by a **-y**, add **-s** to make the plural.

alloy…alloys	day…days	essay…essays
bay…bays	delay…delays	key…keys
boy…boys	display…displays	way…ways

2. When the noun ends in a consonant followed by a **-y**, change the **-y** to **-ies** to make the plural.

analogy…analogies	berry…berries	family…families
army…armies	body…bodies	gypsy…gypsies
baby…babies	city…cities	vacancy…vacancies

Exception: The plural form of **proper nouns**, which are names, that end in a consonant followed by a **-y** is made by just adding **-s.**

February…Februarys	Hello Kitty…Hello Kittys

3. When the noun ends in **ch, s, sh, x**, or **z**, add **-es** to make the plural.

batch…batches	inch…inches	tax…taxes
box…boxes	polish…polishes	waltz…waltzes
class…classes	sinus…sinuses	wish…wishes

Exception: When a word ends in a vowel followed by **z**, the plural is **-zzes**, like:

quiz…quizzes	wiz…wizzes

4. When the noun ends in an **-o**, add **-s** to make the plural.

casino…casinos	photo…photos	studio…studios
disco…discos	radio…radios	turbo…turbos
logo…logos	scenario…scenarios	video…videos

Exception: Some words ending in **-o** make the plural with **-es.**

echo…echoes	potato…potatoes
hero…heroes	tomato…tomatoes

How many of these words can you write in one sentence?

Irregular Plural Nouns

There are also a number of nouns that have an irregular plural form. This means it's more than just adding -s or -es. Countable nouns that have special plural forms are called **irregular plural nouns**. In this section, we'll take a look at some common ones.

1. Generally, when the noun ends in **-f** or **-fe,** change the **-f** or **-fe** to **-ves** to make the plural.

half…halves	life…lives	shelf…shelves
knife…knives	loaf…loaves	thief…thieves
leaf…leaves	self…selves	wife…wives

   Exception: Some words ending in **-f** or **-fe** make the plural with **-s**.

chef…chefs	cream puff…cream puffs	ref…refs
chief…chiefs	giraffe…giraffes	roof…roofs
cliff…cliffs	handcuff…handcuffs	safe…safes

2. Some nouns have an irregular plural form with a different spelling than the singular form.

appendix…appendices	goose…geese	person…people
child…children	man…men	tooth…teeth
foot…feet	mouse…mice	woman…women

   Exception: The usual plural form of *person* is *people*. However, in legal situations like contracts and court documents, it's possible to use *persons*, as in "Several persons of interest were questioned by the detective."

3. Some nouns have an irregular plural form that is the same spelling as the singular form.

deer…deer	scissors…scissors
fish…fish	sheep…sheep

Exercise 3
Now it's your turn to practice.

Are the following sentences correct or incorrect?

1. Aubrey has several fishes in her aquarium.
   Correct ❏ Incorrect ❏
2. In this city, all of the roofs are blue.
   Correct ❏ Incorrect ❏
3. Please put the books and computer mice on the shelves.
   Correct ❏ Incorrect ❏
4. The chef was talking to a people in the restaurant.
   Correct ❏ Incorrect ❏
5. On the farm, we saw some sheep, some calves, and a wolf.
   Correct ❏ Incorrect ❏

Uncountable Nouns

In general, **uncountable nouns** represent things that we don't look at as separate, individual objects. Uncountable nouns include abstract ideas and concepts. You cannot use numbers to count these nouns. Luckily, though, there are no specialty spellings to remember because an uncountable noun doesn't have a plural form. There are also some uncountable nouns that can actually be counted by using a variety of countable words, such as the quantity or the container they are held in, or by using general words like *a piece, a slice, a bag of, a lot of, some,* and so on.

Liquids are uncountable nouns.

ammonia	juice	soda
beer	milk	soup
coffee	oil	tea
gasoline	shampoo	water

You can say things like *a can of beer, two cups of coffee, three bottles of oil,* and *a lot of water.* The exception to this rule is when we talk about drinks. In conversational English, you can say things like:

- I had two beers last night. *It means two bottles of beer.*
- Let's order a few coffees for dessert. *It means a few cups of coffee.*
- I asked the server to bring a couple of waters. *It means a couple of glasses of water.*

Materials are uncountable nouns.

cotton	iron	rubber
fabric	leather	tin
glass	paper	wood
gold	plastic	wool

> You can, however, say things like *a roll of fabric, a piece of plastic*, and *a pile of wood.*

Gases and other natural phenomena are uncountable nouns.

air	hail	smoke
electricity	oxygen	snow
fire	pollution	steam
fog	rain	thunder

> You can, however, say things like *some fog, a container of oxygen*, and *a crack of thunder.*

School subjects and languages are uncountable nouns.

biology	Japanese	math
English	literature	psychology
French		

Abstract concepts, emotions, feelings, and other ideas are uncountable nouns.

adventure	jealousy	romance
beauty	love	sorrow
belief	luck	truth
hope	maturity	wonder

Collective words that represent groups of things, often very small things, are uncountable nouns.

equipment	junk	money
food	livestock	rice
furniture	luggage	salt
grass	mail	traffic

┌─────────────────────────────────┐
│ **Exercise 4** │
│ **Now it's your turn to practice.** │
└─────────────────────────────────┘

Underline the nouns in the sentence and then decide if they are countable
or uncountable.

             C   C   C   U

Example: *We have a _suitcase_, a _backpack_, a shopping _bag_, and some other _luggage_.*

1. The beauty in this wood is shown in the pattern.
2. There is a lot of garbage and junk in the old house.
3. We get a lot of mail. Some is from our customers, but much of it is junk.
4. Viktor has a lot of furniture, including several chairs, tables, and sofas in
   his apartment.
5. All of the beer, wine, and soda is in the cooler.

Nouns That Can Be Both Countable and Uncountable

As you can see, English can be tricky, and this part is no exception. Some nouns can
be both countable and uncountable, depending on the situation and the context.
Here are some examples:

Time

Time is <u>countable</u> when it means experience.

1. We had a nice time at the party.
2. I have been there many times.
3. I told him three times not to be late.

Time is <u>not countable</u> when it means clock time, so we don't say "a time" or "times."

1. I need time to think about your request.
2. It took some time to finish my work.
3. I have no time to play golf this week.

Space

Space is <u>countable</u> when it means an empty area that can be used for something.

1. I have a space in my car to hold a coffee cup.
2. There are a few spaces available to park your car.
3. The conference is sold out, so there are no spaces left.

Space is <u>not countable</u> when it means the universe.

1. Jack studies astronomy because he is interested in space.
2. Do you think there is any intelligent life in space?
3. Will passenger space travel be coming in the next decade?

Experience

Experience is <u>countable</u> when it relates to time.

1. I had several great experiences when I was living overseas.
2. I always have an interesting experience when I hang out with my friends.
3. I've had some funny experiences trying to speak a second language.

Experience is <u>not countable</u> when it means knowledge or skills.

1. Jack has a lot of experience playing golf. He started when he was six years old.
2. Do you have any experience in sales?
3. Doing an internship can give you practical work experience.

Other examples of words that can be either countable or not countable, depending on their context:

| aspirin | coffee | democracy |

Exercise 5
Now it's your turn to practice.

Write original sentences using the nouns *time, space,* and *experience* in both the countable and uncountable forms.

Compound Nouns

A **compound noun** is formed when we put two nouns or a noun and another word together to produce one new meaning. There are three groups of compound nouns.

Group 1

Two words become one word:

blackboard	haircut	sunglasses
bookstore	newspaper	toothpaste
checkout	notebook	watermelon

Group 2

Two words are separated by a space but used together:

bus stop	living room	swimming pool
dinner table	music box	tennis racket
ice cream	oil tank	washing machine

Group 3

Hyphenated nouns are words connected by hyphens. These words are made up of two nouns or a combination of nouns and other words.

first-timer	merry-go-round	six-pack
grown-up	runner-up	son-in-law
high-rise	singer-songwriter	warm-up

Exercise 6
Now it's your turn to practice.

Match each noun in column A with a noun in column B to make a compound noun. Write your answers as one word, two words, or hyphenated words.

A	B	Answer
1. bus	up	
2. coffee	table	
3. living	store	
4. fire	stop	
5. tennis	room	
6. warm	racket	
7. note	drill	
8. book	cup	
9. dinner	book	

Hyphenated Nouns

When we hyphenate nouns and numbers, the resulting combination becomes an adjective, or describing word. Interestingly, the noun part of these adjectives is always singular. When we say that Amisha is twenty years old, *years* is plural because *year* is a countable noun, and since twenty is more than one, we say *twenty years*. But when we say that Amisha is a twenty-year-old woman, hyphenating the words *twenty, year,* and *old* turns the resulting phrase into an adjective. Now the noun *year* is in the singular form: Amisha is a *twenty-year-old* woman. *Twenty-year-old* is a hyphenated adjective.

Here are some other examples:

1. Kim bought a *ten-pound* bag of flour to make cookies.
2. All the doctors work a *twelve-hour* shift two or three times per month.
3. Chang has a *thirty-six-inch* monitor on his desk.

When you need to use one of these hyphenated adjectives, the plural is formed by changing the noun and not the hyphenated phrase.

1. Kim bought *four ten-pound bag**s*** of flour to make cookies.
2. The doctor had to work *two twelve-hour shift**s*** this week.
3. The stockbroker has *three thirty-six-inch monitor**s*** on his desk.

Fractions are also written as hyphenated numbers.

1. The factory experienced a *one-third* cut in orders last year.
2. You should fill those cupcake tins *two-thirds* full.
3. If you cut *three-sixteenths* of an inch from that pipe, it should fit perfectly.

Exercise 7
Now it's your turn to practice.

Rewrite the nouns in the following sentences using a hyphenated adjective.

1. Refund policy: You have seven days to return the item. *It's a* .... *refund policy.*
2. The conference took three days. *It was a* .... *conference.*
3. The box weighs twenty pounds. *It's a* .... *box.*

Capitalization

Nouns that represent names are called **proper nouns**, which are different from the common nouns we've covered. Proper nouns are always capitalized. These proper nouns include the following groups:

Group 1

Names of days, months, and holidays:

Chinese New Year	July	Monday
Christmas	March	Saturday
January	Memorial Day	Tuesday

Group 2

Names of places, nationalities, languages, and religions:

American	Dutch	Mexican
Canada	Islam	Siberia
Christianity	Judaism	Tokyo

Group 3

Names of people, their titles, and names of organizations:

Dr. Christopher	Marta	The Red Cross
Ms. Dubois	Microsoft	Professor Smirnov
Benjamin Franklin	Anna Parsons	Volkswagen

> **Exercise 8**
> **Now it's your turn to practice.**

Rewrite the sentences using capital letters as needed.

1. There is going to be a presentation on the first three presidents of the united states on monday, january 3.
2. Bill gates is the founder of microsoft.
3. The amazon river in south america is the second-longest river in the world.
4. We watched the hollywood classic *gone with the wind* in my social studies class today.

Determiners

English nouns are interesting. They tend to get lonely, and in most cases, nouns like a friend to be with them. We'll call that friend a **determiner**. Determiners, words like *a, the, that,* and *her,* tell us which noun we're talking about by introducing and identifying it. They help identify the noun within the context of the sentence, paragraph, or conversation.

The most common determiners are **articles**. There are three articles in English: *a, an*, and *the*. *A* and *an* are called **indefinite articles**, and *the* is called a **definite article**. Let's look at a few examples:

1. I have *a* pen.
2. Jenny ate *an* apple.
3. We went to *the* park on Main Street.

Do you see how *a* pen and *an* apple could be any pen or apple? They're indefinite. But *the* park on Main Street—it's clear which park we're talking about; *the* makes it definite.

We also use **possessive nouns** and **possessive adjectives** as determiners. Words like *Tasha's, Toyota's,* and *Italy's* are possessive nouns. Words like *my, her,* and *their* are possessive adjectives.

1. *Tasha's* cat is so cute!
2. *Toyota's* job interviews are very challenging.
3. *Italy's* flag is green, white, and red.
4. Have you ever seen *my* car?
5. She was telling me about *her* job.
6. *Their* house is on the corner of *their* block.

Demonstrative pronouns like *this, that, these,* and *those* can also be used as determiners.

1. *This* coffee is really good.
2. How much is *that* laptop?
3. Have you tried *these* cookies?
4. I have never seen *those* books before.

Other words, such as **quantifiers**, are also used as determiners. These are words like *each, every, some, any, many,* and *much*.

1. The teacher gave *each* student a pen.
2. We need to put *every* chair in the closet.
3. I ordered *some* sandwiches for lunch.
4. Do you have *any* pencils?
5. There are *many* people in the room.
6. I didn't get *much* sleep last night.

Exercise 9
Now it's your turn to practice.

In the following sentences, decide what, if anything, should go in the blank space.

1. There is _____ man at _____ front desk in _____ lobby who can help _____ you.
2. I think we need to buy _____ new TV. _____ one in _____ living room is broken.
3. We met Jane's _____ husband and _____ son at _____ party last night.
4. My sister told me that _____ Franco's is the best French restaurant in _____ city.
5. Can you ask _____ boss if we can go _____ home early tomorrow?

Using *a* and *an*

We use *a* and *an* with singular countable nouns. When the noun begins with a consonant sound, use *a*. When the singular countable noun begins with a vowel sound, use *an*.

Most nouns that begin with a consonant sound have a consonant as the first letter.

1. She has a cat, a dog, a fish, and a monkey.
2. A man and a woman went to a park near a river.

But sometimes a noun that begins with a consonant sound actually has a vowel as the first letter. This happens with some words that begin with *eu*, *o*, and *u* as shown here—they all sound like they start with a *y*.

1. A unicorn wearing a uniform made a U-turn on a unicycle.
2. A European found a euro near a UFO at the university.

Most nouns that begin with a vowel sound have a vowel as the first letter.

1. I bought an apple, an egg, and an onion.
2. An usher left an umbrella near an academy.

But sometimes a noun that begins with a vowel sound actually has a consonant as the first letter. This happens with some words that begin with *h*, as shown here.

1. I was there for an hour.
2. He is an heir to the throne.

We tend to use *a*, *an*, or no article (Ø) when we talk about things in general. Look at the following example:

I like bananas. Bananas are delicious and also a good source of vitamins. Bananas are also one of the most inexpensive fruits. I usually eat a banana in the morning with my breakfast.

You'll notice that I used the plural form of *banana* the first three times. That's because we tend to use the plural form of countable nouns when we make generalizations. When I say that I like bananas and that bananas are delicious, I'm speaking about bananas in general and not any particular banana. In the last sentence, I said that I eat a banana in the morning. I said *a banana* because I'm talking about a single banana.

**Exercise 10
Now it's your turn to practice.**

Write *a*, *an*, or Ø in the following blanks.

1. We are staying at _____ hotel on the beach.
2. Sorry, but I really don't like _____ football.
3. I would rather listen to _____ music than watch _____ TV program.
4. Frida likes _____ art, so we went to _____ art gallery.

Using *the*

The is a **definite article**. We call it that because we use *the* to talk about something definite and specific.

We use *the* before a noun when we believe the listener/reader knows exactly what noun we're talking about. There are typically three situations in which this can happen. First, it's because we've already mentioned it.

1. I saw a cat and a dog. **The** cat was brown, and **the** dog was black and white.
2. I went to a party last night. **The** party was a lot of fun.
3. Jan has a boy and a girl. **The** girl is three, and she's adorable!

Second, it's because there is only one.

1. **The** president of **the** company is going to speak at **the** annual meeting.
2. Look at **the** moon! It's full tonight.
3. I'd like to speak to **the** manager, please.

Lastly, it's because it's the usual place that you go or the usual item you use or because it's clear from the context or situation.

1. I went to **the** post office this morning.
2. My mom was cooking in **the** kitchen all day.
3. Who is **the** woman standing by **the** window?

Let's explore some other special cases in which we use *the*.

With a **superlative adjective**, we use *the* because there is only one. That's because superlative adjectives are used to communicate an extreme comparison, like *the tallest, the oldest, the best*, etc.

1. Marco is **the** tallest player on the team.
2. Contrary to popular belief, the Brooklyn Bridge is not **the** oldest bridge in New York City.

When we say something in general about an entire species or a type of thing:

1. **The** koala bear is native to Australia.
2. **The** brain is the control tower of the body.

When we talk about musical instruments:

1. Sergei plays **the** guitar really well.
2. My sister is learning **the** piano now.

When we refer to a system or service:

1. How do you spend your time on **the** train?
2. I love to listen to that program on **the** radio*.
3. I really think you should tell **the** police about it.

   Exception: We say ***the*** *radio,* ***the*** *news,* and ***the*** *Internet,* but sometimes we say *television (TV)* without *the*.

When we use adjectives like *rich, poor, elderly,* and *unemployed* to talk about groups of people:

1. This organization provides services to **the** poor.
2. Many people insist that **the** rich pay more taxes.
3. Frances works for an NGO that helps **the** disabled.

   Exception: We do not use *the* before races. For example, we wouldn't say *the whites* or *the blacks*.

These are some special cases regarding *the*. We use *the* with:

Acronyms for organizations: the FBI, the CIA, the KGB, the UK

Cinemas and theaters, hotels and restaurants, and museums: the Taj Mahal, the Shubert Theater, the Hilton Hotel, the Rainbow Room, the Metropolitan Museum, the Colosseum

Countries whose names contain *of* or words like *kingdom, republic, or states*: the United States of America, the People's Republic of China, the United Kingdom

Countries whose names are a plural noun: the Netherlands, the Philippines, the Bahamas

Families: the Lees, the Patels, the Russos

Natural and geographical places, like deserts, groups of islands, mountain ranges, rivers, seas, and oceans: the Sahara Desert, the Canary Islands, the Swiss Alps, the Amazon River, the Atlantic Ocean

Newspapers: *The Times of India, The Japan Times, The Washington Post*

Organizations: the Trevor Project, the United Nations, the Teamsters Union

Ships and other vehicles: the *Queen Mary*, the bullet train, the *Mayflower*

We **do not** use *the* with:

Acronyms pronounced as a word: NASA, LASER, NATO, SCUBA

Airports, stadiums, and other public buildings: Dulles Airport, Fenway Park, City Hall

Diseases and illnesses: Alzheimer's disease, Parkinson's disease, HIV

Lakes: Lake Geneva, Lake Como, Lake Michigan

Names of people, cities, and towns: George Washington, Helsinki, Mayberry

Schools and universities: Princeton University, Trinity College, Oxford University

Titles of books, movies, and plays: *War and Peace, Casablanca, Hamlet*

Exceptions:

Cities that have *the* in the name: The Plains, Virginia; The Bronx, New York; The Hague, the Netherlands

Restaurants, bars, and retail shops that have the owner's name in them: Joe's Pub, McSorley's Ale House, Cartier Jewelers, Saks Fifth Avenue

Some companies: The Art of Shaving, The Kraft Group, The Limited, The Walt Disney Company

---

Exercise 11
Now it's your turn to practice.

Answer the questions, with careful use of *a*, *an*, *the*, and Ø.

1. What pet do you have? (Think of your pet, or imagine that you have a pet. Tell us who has the pet, what kind of pet it is, and what color it is.)

   I have ....

2. What do you think of when you see the stars, the moon, or the sun?

   When I see ....

3. Which room of your house do you like the best? Answer that and also write about one or two of your favorite things in that room.

   I prefer .... *In that room, I really like* ....

4. What music do you like? Write about that and also write about a musical instrument that you like to listen to or one that you would like to play.

   I like ....

5. Where do your neighbors or friends like to go? Write about some of your neighbors or friends, using their family name. Mention which attractions in your city (museums, theaters, historical places, etc.) they like to go.

   My friends ....

Possessive Adjectives

The next type of determiner is the **possessive adjective**. These are *his, her, my, your, our, their, its, whose,* and *one's*. We use possessive adjectives before a noun, just like in the case of *a, an,* and *the*. These words describe to whom the noun belongs or with whom the noun is associated.

1. Have you seen *my* pen?
2. *Your* hair looks nice today.
3. I spent an hour looking for *their* house.
4. Do you know *whose* dog this is?
5. Sometimes it isn't easy solving *one's* problems alone.

Possessive adjectives are used as determiners before a noun, so we don't use them with other determiners. You can say "This is *my* pen" but not "This is *the my* pen."

Sometimes, when we talk about what happens to a person's body, like an injury or an illness, we use articles instead of possessive adjectives.

1. During the storm, the tree branch fell and hit Jay on *the* head.
2. Her CAT scan showed a spot on *the* lungs.
3. He fell when the ball hit him on *the* back.

However, when we're just talking about a person's body and not what happens to it, we use possessive adjectives.

1. There was a snake sitting on *her* shoulders.
2. He has two puppies on *his* lap.
3. I was sitting on the sofa with *my* eyes closed, listening to the music.

Awkward Mistakes to Avoid
Don't Press Send!

Is it *him and I,* or is it *him and me*?

Many of us, even native English speakers, were incorrectly trained to write *him and I* or *her and I,* but it should actually be *him/her/them and* **me**. This common mistake occurs when there is more than one object pronoun. To make sure you've got things right, experiment by removing the other pronoun: "Bring that pizza to him and I" wouldn't work if you took out *him*. ("Bring that pizza to I" is incorrect.) "Bring that pizza to him and **me**" is correct.

Fill in the blank with the correct possessive adjective or other determiner (*a, an, the*) as necessary. Write Ø if none is needed.

1. I can't find _____ pen, so can I borrow _____ pen or pencil?
2. I saw Daniela today. The stylist did a great job on _____ hair.
3. Diego had _____ shoulder pain because he got hit in _____ shoulder playing softball.

Demonstrative Pronouns

This, these, that, and *those*—which are **demonstrative pronouns**—make up the final set of determiners. We can use these four words before a noun and in place of a noun.

We use demonstrative pronouns before nouns that represent both people and things.

1. **This** book will help you with your English.
2. **These** students have been working very hard.
3. **That** woman is the CEO of this company.
4. **Those** cars were made before World War II.

We typically use *this* and *these* when we talk about people and things near the speaker. We use *that* and *those* when we talk about people and things far from the speaker.

1. **This** coffee mug is my favorite.
2. Can you put **these** books on the shelf?
3. Have you been to **that** restaurant before?
4. Look at the line in front of the theater! **Those** people have been waiting a long time.

We also use *this* and *these* when we talk about situations that are happening now or going to happen soon. We use *that* and *those* when we talk about situations that happened already.

1. **This** movie is going to be fun.
2. **These** training meetings can be boring.
3. **That** was a delicious pizza.
4. I think **those** days in high school were a lot of fun.

Decide whether the following sentences are correct or incorrect. If the sentence is incorrect, write the sentence correctly.

1. I think these are the best cookies I've ever eaten.
2. That is a great party! Don't you love this music?
3. You should go there. I've been to this restaurant many times. You'll love it.
4. This employees have worked very hard this month.
5. Look at this photo from college. Do you remember that girls?

Quantifiers

Quantifiers are words like *some*, *both*, and *many* that come before a noun to express the quantity of the noun. Let's explore these types of modifiers and how they work.

Some and *Any*

The words *some* and *any* are used before nouns to talk about an indefinite quantity or amount. We use *some* and *any* when we don't need to say exactly how much or how many of a thing there is. We use *some* and *any* before plural countable nouns and uncountable nouns. *Some* is used in positive sentences. *Any* is used in negative sentences and in questions.

1. I put **some** Parmesan cheese on my pizza, and it was delicious.
2. I have **some** time tomorrow for a meeting. How does your schedule look?
3. We don't have **any** milk, so we can't make pancakes.
4. Do you have **any** ideas for Anika's birthday?

When we use a determiner before a noun, we use *some of* and *any of*.

1. I'm going to use **some of** the eggs to make a cake.
2. I met **some of** her friends at a party.
3. I don't believe **any of** those students actually studied.
4. Would **any of** your friends like a cat?

It's also possible to use *some* and *any* without a noun.

1. Let me know if you have **any** extra sunscreen. I need **some**.
2. The donuts in the conference room are homemade. Have you had **any**?

We also use *some* followed by a singular noun when talking about an unknown person or thing.

1. **Some** guy on the train stepped on my foot.
2. Min got a job with **some** tech company in Silicon Valley.

Some is also used in a sentence or a question to offer something.

1. If you'd like **some** help with your homework, call me.
2. Would you like **some** tea or coffee for dessert?

Exercise 14
Now it's your turn to practice.

Write *some* or *any* in the blanks.

1. Why don't you put _____ sugar or maple syrup on your oatmeal?
2. Do you have _____ time to have a meeting tomorrow?
3. Would you like _____ mustard or ketchup on your fries?
4. I need _____ hair wax. Do you have _____?
5. Here are the exam results. _____ of you passed the exam, and _____ of you didn't. If you have _____ questions about your grades, come see me after class.

Each and *Every*

Each and *every* are used to refer to people or things in a group that we refer to separately. *Each* and *every* are followed by a singular, countable noun. Generally, we can use *each* and *every* interchangeably, especially when we talk about time.

1. Ahmed works hard **each** day.
2. Ahmed works hard **every** day.
3. **Each** year, we get older and wiser.
4. **Every** year, we get older and wiser.

We tend to use *each* when we think of things individually or separately. There may be a group of things or people, and we use *each* when we think about them on an individual basis.

1. **Each** pen has the company logo on it. (This means that the pens, one by one, have the company logo.)
2. **Each** student will have an opportunity to talk to the teacher. (This means that the students, one by one, can talk to the teacher.)

However, we tend to use *every* when we think of things as part of a group, similar to the way we use *all*.

1. **Every** person on the tour receives a map and a rain hat.
2. **Every** guest at the party had fun.

We also use *each*, and not *every*, when we talk about two things.

1. Jim has a bottle of water in **each** hand.
2. Married life is sometimes not easy. **Each** person needs to compromise sometimes.

We also use *each*, and not *every*, before the preposition *of*.

1. **Each** of these pens has the company logo on it.
2. **Each** of you should follow me.

We use *every* when we talk about clock time.

1. The bus comes **every** hour.
2. **Every** ten minutes the phone rang.

Exercise 15
Now it's your turn to practice.

Decide if the following sentences are correct or incorrect. If the sentence is incorrect, write the sentence correctly.

1. He gets a checkup at the doctor's office each six months.
2. Each of you can have a cookie.
3. I'm going to give a booklet to every person in the room.
4. The clown balanced a bottle on every foot.
5. Every time he saw her, he fell more deeply in love with her.

Many, Much, and a Lot of

We use *much* and *many* to refer to a large amount or quantity of people and things. We use *many* before countable nouns, and we use *much* before uncountable nouns. *Many* indicates a large number of things, and *much* indicates a large amount of something.

1. I have **many** ideas for the weekend.
2. **Many** people in the United States like to eat pizza.
3. I don't have **much** time this week.
4. Did you do **much** research on this subject?

Many is used in positive statements, negative statements, and questions.

1. I have **many** ideas for the weekend.
2. José just moved to Milwaukee and doesn't have **many** friends.
3. Do you have **many** books and CDs?

Many and *much* can also be used in a positive sentence with a modifier like *so* or *too*.

1. There were so **many** people on the train this morning.
2. I had too **many** cups of coffee this morning. I really need to cut down.
3. There was too **much** snow last winter.
4. I am so happy that we have so **much** time to spend together.

Much is generally used in negative statements and questions. For positive statements, we don't usually use *much* by itself. We prefer using *a lot of* instead of *much*.

1. I don't have **much** time this week.
2. Do you have **much** work to do this week?
3. I think we'll have **a lot of** snow this winter. (We can't say *I think we will have* **much** *snow this winter.*)

A lot of can be used before uncountable nouns and plural countable nouns in statements and questions.

1. I have **a lot of** ideas for the weekend.
2. I don't have **a lot of** time this week.
3. Do you have **a lot of** experience with that software?

Write *much* or *many* in the blanks. Write *a lot of* if you can't use *much* or *many*.

1. Gregor doesn't have _____ friends, even though he's lived here a year.
2. I don't think we have _____ time to visit that museum.
3. There was _____ rain last month, and that's why we have so _____ flowers.
4. I think too _____ people don't realize how _____ effort it takes to run a business.
5. The rooms in this house have so _____ space.

A Few and a Little

Overview: We use *a few* and *a little* to refer to a small amount or quantity of people and things. We use *a few* before plural countable nouns, like *a few pens* or *a few chairs*. We use *a little* before noncountable nouns, like *a little water* or *a little time*.

A Few and a Little

A few and *a little* have a positive connotation. Using *a* before *few* and *little* shows that there's a small amount but that we're satisfied with that amount.

1. I have **a few** friends who are English teachers.
2. There are **a few** peaches in the fridge. Why don't you try one?
3. I have **a little** free time, so I'm going shopping before work.

Few and Little

On the other hand, *few* and *little* (without *a*) have a negative connotation. *Few* and *little* (without *a*) indicate that the amount is not enough and that we're not satisfied with that.

1. **Few** people get the chance to meet a celebrity. That's too bad.
2. There are **few** pens left. We need to order some.
3. There's **little** time to prepare for the exam. I wish there was more.
4. There's **little** milk left, so it's not enough for a bowl of cereal.

Decide if the sentence is correct based on the usage of (*a*) *few* and (*a*) *little*.

1. Roberto has a few good ideas for marketing our products, so I think we'll sell a lot.
2. I have so much to do but so a little time. I don't think I can manage.
3. There was little rain over the weekend so we had a great time camping.
4. I've saved a few money, so I can finally get that new laptop.

Chapter Two

Adjectives

Adjectives are words we use to describe nouns. We use adjectives before nouns and after the *be* verb (page 59) without nouns. A car is just a car until we add some adjectives— the **sleek**, **red sports** car is much more fun to think about!

Using adjectives before a noun like *car* is the easy way to use an adjective. But we can also use adjectives with the *be* verb and verbs like *feel, seem, look,* etc.

1. I am **glad** you like your present.
2. I feel **tired**, so I'm going to take a nap.
3. It seems **cold** outside. Please bundle up.

We use adjectives to give more information about nouns and situations. In English, we usually use the adjective *before* the noun.

1. He has a **new** pen.
2. We had a **delicious** pizza.

We tend to use adjectives *after* measurement nouns.

1. The pond in Central Park is about one foot **deep**.
2. My sister is two years **younger** than me.

With *so* and *such,* we use *so* followed by an adjective and *such* followed by a noun phrase, which is a noun preceded by an adjective (like *warm day* and *nice guy*).

1. It's **so** warm today. → It's **such** a warm day.
2. He's **so** nice. → He's **such** a nice guy.

We use *nice and* followed by an adjective to show that something or someone is comfortable or pleasant.

1. Mom's chicken soup will make you feel **nice and** warm.
2. We got to the airport **nice and** early, so we had a drink in the lounge.

Exercise 18
Now it's your turn to practice.

Try out this funny word game.

A. Write an adjective that represents age (ex.: new, old, modern, etc.).

....

B. Write an adjective that represents a quality (ex.: good, terrible, fancy, etc.).

....

C. Write an adjective that represents how food tastes (ex: yummy, delicious, sour, etc.). ....

D. Write an adjective that represents a color (ex.: blue, tan, red, etc.).

....

E. Write an adjective that represents a shape (ex.: square, round, triangular, etc.).

....

F. Write a number. ....

G. Write another adjective that represents a quality (ex.: good, terrible, fancy, etc.).

....

Now, read the story, inserting the words you just wrote:

Zhang Li decided to cook dinner. He bought an ....A............ cookbook that has ....B.............. recipes. When he saw a recipe for chicken soup, he thought to himself, *This looks* ....C............... So he went to the store and got some nice ....D.............. carrots and a nice ....E.............. onion. Then he went home and cooked the soup. He made a mistake with the time and ended up cooking the soup ....F.............. hours longer than he should have. His family thought the soup was ....G...............

Attributive and Predicative Adjectives

Attributive adjectives can only be used before a noun, and **predicative adjectives** can only be used after a noun.

Some common attributive adjectives are *chief, elder, main, total,* and *utter.*

1. You can say *the chief advisor,* but not *the advisor is chief.*
2. You can say *his elder sister,* but not *his sister is elder.*
3. You can say *the main office,* but not *the office is main.*
4. You can say *this is the total price,* but not *the price is total.*
5. You can say *he is an utter fool,* but not *he is utter.*

Some common predicative adjectives are *afraid, alive, ashamed, asleep,* and *aware.*

1. You can say *the children were afraid,* but not *the afraid children.*
2. You can say *the plants are alive,* but not *the alive plants.*
3. You can say *the man was ashamed,* but not *the ashamed man.*
4. You can say *the dog is asleep,* but not *the asleep dog.*
5. You can say *the workers were aware,* but not *the aware workers.*

Decide if the adjectives in the following sentences are used correctly. If the adjective is incorrect, write the sentence correctly.

1. A toaster is *useful* something to have in the kitchen.
2. We need to find someone *experienced* to do this job.
3. In the story, the characters live at the bottom of the *deep, blue* sea.
4. She told me that she has a suitcase *big* for her trip to Europe.
5. There was an *asleep* child on the sofa.

The Order of Adjectives

When two or more adjectives come before a noun, we put them in a particular order. The order is first based on whether the adjective is classifying or describing the noun. Classifying means putting something in a category.

Some adjectives used to classify a noun include:

building blocks   **medieval** castle   **portable** computer
financial advice   **musical** instrument   **running** shoes
medical equipment   **political** party

Some adjectives used to describe a noun include:

comfortable shoes   **new** computer
glass decanter   **popular** party
good advice   **small** blocks
modern physics   **sophisticated** equipment

We put descriptive adjectives before classifying adjectives.

comfortable running shoes   **new portable** computer
good financial advice   **popular political** party
modern quantum physics   **sophisticated medical** equipment

Opinions generally come before facts, and we tend to put commas between three or more adjectives.

good, accurate financial advice   **sophisticated, modern medical**
inexpensive, wooden building blocks equipment
popular, new political party

Descriptive adjectives generally go in this order: size, age, shape, color, origin, and material.

Visha has a **small, old, round, black, Japanese wooden** box.

Although the sentence you just read illustrates the order of descriptive adjectives, more than two or three adjectives can sound awkward or forced.

José has **comfortable, old, blue, nylon running** shoes.

Exercise 20
Now it's your turn to practice.

1. How many nouns can you use after the following adjectives?

Medical:
Portable:
Glass:

2. Take one of the adjective sets you made in the first exercise and try to make a complete set of adjectives using size, age, shape, color, origin, and material.

Adjective Comparisons

We use adjectives when we compare nouns. We use the **comparative form** of adjectives when we compare two things and the **superlative form** of adjectives when we compare more than two things.

The comparative and superlative forms of adjectives are made depending on the number of syllables in the adjective. For adjectives with one syllable (one vowel sound), like *big, low*, and *small*, add **-er** to make the comparative form and add **-est** to make the superlative form.

big…bigger…biggest   high…higher…highest
clean…cleaner…cleanest   low…lower…lowest
fat…fatter…fattest   quick…quicker…quickest

For adjectives with more than one syllable, use *more* to make the comparative form and *the most* to make the superlative form.

careful…more careful…most careful
difficult…more difficult…most difficult
important…more important…most important
intelligent…more intelligent…most intelligent
peaceful…more peaceful…most peaceful
thoughtful…more thoughtful…most thoughtful

For adjectives ending in **-y**, change the **-y** to **-ier** to make the comparative form, and change **-y** to **-iest** to make the superlative form.

angry…angrier…angriest   dusty…dustier…dustiest
busy…busier…busiest   happy…happier…happiest
comfy…comfier…comfiest   pretty…prettier…prettiest

**Exercise 21
Now it's your turn to practice.**

Look around the room you're in right now. Find three objects. Using the three patterns you just learned, first compare two of the things, and then compare all three things.

Participle Adjectives

Participle adjectives are formed from the *ed* and *ing* participles of verbs. Examples include:

amaze…amazed…amazing
amuse…amused…amusing
bore…bored…boring
disappoint…disappointed…disappointing
excite…excited…exciting
interest…interested…interesting

We use adjectives ending in **-ed** to describe how a person feels about something.

1. Everyone was *amazed* at the robot's ability.
2. Huang was *excited* when he won the lottery!
3. I'm *interested* in jazz.

We use adjectives ending in **-ing** to describe the reason a person has a certain feeling.

1. The robot's ability is *amazing*.
2. Winning the lottery is *exciting*.
3. Jazz is a very *interesting* style of music.

We can also use **-ing** adjectives to describe a person's character or personality.

1. The CEO is an *interesting* man.
2. My history teacher is *boring*.

Exercise 22
Now it's your turn to practice.

Write some sentences based on the following prompts.

1. An interesting place in your town: "*The Museum of Modern Art is interesting because…*"
2. An amazing person you know
3. An exciting trip you'd like to take
4. The last time you were bored
5. Something you are very interested in

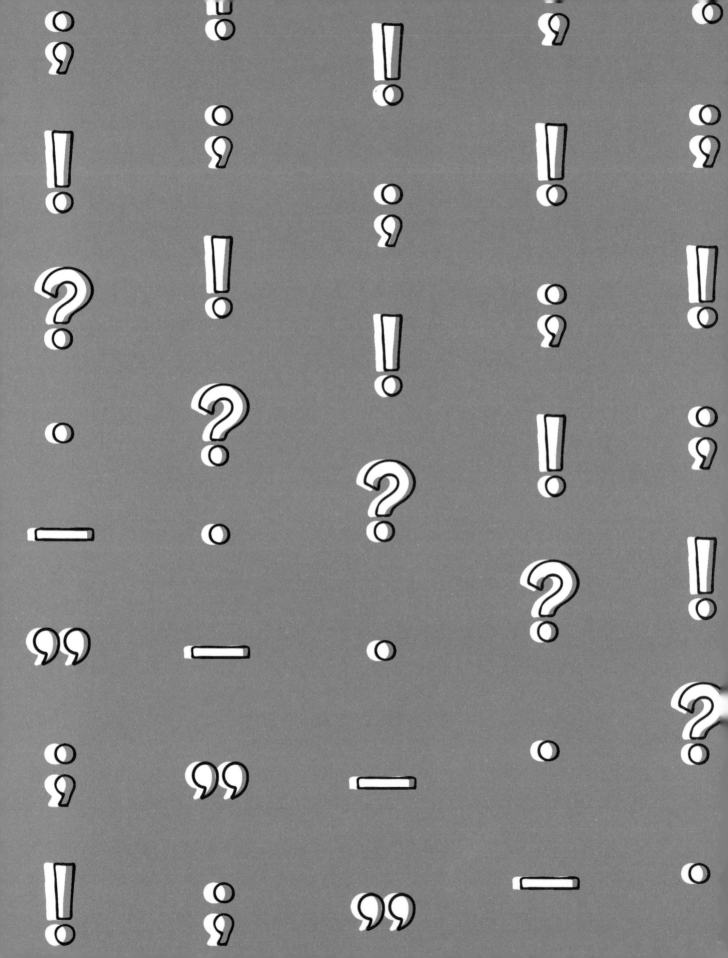

Chapter Three

Adverbs

Adverbs are words that usually modify a verb, adjective, or other part of speech. I'd bet money that if I asked 10 people on the street to name an adverb, they'd say a word that ended in *-ly—quickly, happily, carefully*. They'd be right. But there are more adverbs that don't end in *-ly*, and we'll explore what they are and how they're used.

Adverbs of Manner and Place

We use **adverbs of manner** to describe how something is done or how it happens.

beautifully	hard	slowly
fast	loudly	softly
happily	nicely	well

Adverbs of place, which describe where an action is taking place, don't have any particular spelling conventions. Some examples include:

abroad	here	somewhere
anywhere	inside	there
downtown	outside	uptown

Adverbs of manner and place usually go at the end of a sentence, but some adverbs ending in **-ly** can also come before the verb.

1. Your sister plays the piano **beautifully** (cannot be *Your sister beautifully plays the piano*.).
2. The boy **gently** petted the cat (can also be *The boy petted the cat gently*.).
3. Some of the employees are going to work **overseas**.
4. Lynn can speak several languages, but she's never been **abroad**.

Some adverbs of place, particularly *here* and *there*, can come at the beginning of a sentence. You'll notice that the word order is *here/there* → verb → subject. If the subject is a pronoun, the word order is *here/there* → pronoun → verb.

1. **Here** comes Amir. Let's sing "Happy Birthday" to him.
2. **Here** he comes. Let's sing "Happy Birthday" to him.
3. **There** goes the train. I knew we should have left for the station earlier.
4. **There** it goes. I knew we should have left for the station earlier.

The usual order for adverbs is manner, place, and then time.

1. We work **hard here every day**.
2. He left **early yesterday**.

Use the adverbs and the word clues to write sentences.

quietly / nicely / downtown / hard / abroad / outside

Example: teacher / speaks / the: The teacher speaks quietly.

1. was / last / it / Sunday / snowing ....
2. day / go / it's / a / so / let's / nice ....
3. and / it's / live / to / work / challenging ....
4. play / children / the / together ....
5. I / you / get / will / when / call / I ....

Adverbs of Time

We use **adverbs of time** to describe when something's done or when it happens. There are two types. The first is **adverbs of indefinite frequency**. The most common are *always, often, usually, sometimes, occasionally, hardly ever, rarely, seldom*, and *never*. The other type is **adverbs of definite frequency**. These are more precise, such as *once a week, every day, on the weekend, three times a month*, etc.

There are four basic patterns for adverbs of time. Adverbs of indefinite frequency go before the verb, unless the verb is the *be* verb (page 59), in which case it goes after.

1. I **often** go to the gym.
2. Tasha **always** drinks coffee.
3. The gym is **usually** open early.
4. The trains in New York City are **rarely** on time.

Adverbs of indefinite frequency go between the auxiliary (helping) verb and main verb.

1. We can **typically** find reasonable prices.
2. Giuseppe has **never** drunk white wine.
3. You'll **rarely** see an on-time train in New York City.

The adverbs *sometimes, often, occasionally, frequently, usually*, and *normally* are exceptions. You might remember them with this acronym: SOOFUN. These are pretty flexible. We could say:

1. **Sometimes**, Giuseppe visits his customers in Chicago.
2. Giuseppe visits his customers in Chicago **sometimes**.
3. Giuseppe **sometimes** visits his customers in Chicago.

Adverbs of definite frequency can go at either the beginning or the end of a sentence.

1. I go to the gym **three times a week**.
2. **Once a month** we go to the movies.
3. Tasha drinks coffee **every day**.

Exercise 24
Now it's your turn to practice.

Using these adverbs, write sentences about what you do.

1. Once a week _____
2. Never _____
3. Sometimes _____
4. Usually _____
5. Every day _____

Other Types and Positions of Adverbs

Some adverbs have other functions, like to show emphasis or focus or to describe probability or completeness. These adverbs go before the word that they modify. Some examples of **emphasis adverbs** are *almost, extremely, just, really*, and *very*. **Focus adverbs** include *also, either, even, mainly, mostly, neither*, and *only*. **Probability adverbs** include *certainly, clearly, definitely, maybe, perhaps*, and *probably*. **Adverbs of completeness** include *completely, hardly, nearly, partly*, and *partially*.

1. I **almost** missed the train.
2. The boss was **extremely** happy with the sales results last month.
3. Iman **even** speaks Thai!
4. The CEO is **also** the company founder.
5. I **definitely** want to see that movie.
6. It was **partly** cloudy all day.

Exercise 25
Now it's your turn to practice.

Answer the questions using a full sentence including the adverb.

1. **Recently**, have you **almost** missed a class, work, a train, or a bus?
2. You can speak English. What language do you **also** speak?
3. What is something you **hardly** do?
4. What is **certainly** the best restaurant in your town?

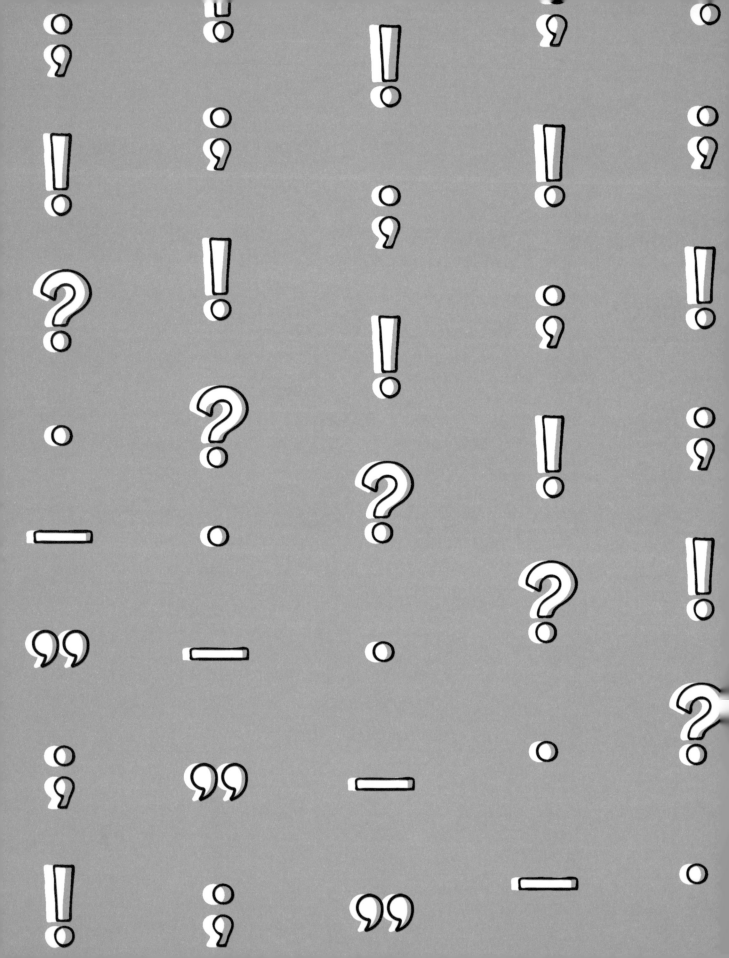

Chapter Four

Verbs

In short, **verbs** are the doing words. They describe the action. The Merriam-Webster dictionary notes, among other traits, that a verb is the "act, occurrence, or mode of being." *Beware! Stop! Go. Run. Pray. Sit. Eat.* These complete sentences stand alone just fine with their lone word—a verb. But not every verb is expected to *run* or *stop*—some verbs are more subtle. Let's explore.

Active versus Stative Verbs

The two types of verbs in English are active and stative. **Active verbs** describe action and movement, like *work*, *study*, *type*, and *walk*. The action can even be a rather inactive one, like *sleep*, *sit*, and *relax*. **Stative verbs** describe a state or condition, like *love*, *feel*, *agree*, and *suppose*.

Active verbs can be used in the progressive form when we indicate actions and movement happening now.

1. Jeff is **working** on the meeting report.
2. The professor is **writing** on the board.
3. I can't chat now. I'm **studying** for the psychology final.

Stative verbs are typically not used in the progressive form when we indicate a state or condition existing now.

1. Tasha **loves** this pizza.
2. That **smells** amazing. What are you cooking?
3. I **agree** with your idea, but I think we should ask the manager first.

Some verbs can be used in both an active and stative way, but when they are used in a progressive form, the meaning is slightly different.

Feel refers to how our senses react to the environment or our body condition.

I **feel** great because I just landed a new job.

Feel is also a special stative verb because we can use it in the progressive with the same meaning.

I'm **feeling** great because I just landed a new job.

On the other hand, **feeling** is similar to **touching** and refers to trying to make physical contact with something.

I'm **feeling** the edge of this cup to check if there are any cracks or chips.

Smell refers to noticing an aroma or odor.

I **smell** pizza. Who brought the pizza into the office? Can I have some?

Smelling refers to using our nose to check the aroma of something.

Sophia: What are you doing?

Liam: I'm **smelling** this pizza to make sure it's not too garlicky. It **smells** good.

Taste refers to the reaction of our tongue to something we put in our mouth.

This alligator **tastes** like chicken.

Tasting refers to using your tongue to sample the flavor of something.

> **Olivia:** What are you doing?

> **Jackson:** I'm **tasting** the soup. I think it needs more salt.

Awkward Mistakes to Avoid
Don't Press Send!

The question of *affect* versus *effect* causes confusion among native speakers and English learners alike. Both words have a verb and noun form. *Affect* can either mean "to influence" (verb) or "an emotional expression" (noun). *Effect* can mean either "to make happen" (verb) or "an impact" (noun). Most of the time, you can assume that *affect* is a verb ("Eating that old pizza really *affected* my stomach") and that *effect* is a noun ("Wow, the pizza really had an *effect* on Tasha!").

Exercise 26
Now it's your turn to practice.

Choose the correct form of the verb.

1. What (are you working / do you work) on today?
2. I (have / am having) a lot of things to bring to the conference.
3. Since everyone (is agreeing / agrees) with the terms, let's sign the contract.
4. I (study / am studying) hard because final exams start tomorrow.
5. This cookie (tastes / is tasting) a bit too sweet.

Verbs Followed by Gerunds

Generally, verbs are followed by a direct object, such as *I like coffee*. But sometimes a verb can be followed either by a **gerund** (an -*ing* verb that functions as a noun), such as *cooking*, or by an **infinitive** (a verb preceded by *to*), like *to cook*, with no difference in meaning.

Here are some of the more common ones:

begin	hate	love
continue	like	prefer

Here are some examples:

1. I like cooking.
2. I like to cook.
3. Aria continued working past 9:00 p.m.
4. Aria continued to work past 9:00 p.m.

There are some verbs that can only be followed by a gerund. Here are the most common:

advise	dislike	practice
allow	finish	prohibit
avoid	keep	quit
can't help	mention	recall
can't stand	mind	regret
complete	miss	try

Here are some examples:

1. The boss **advised bringing** a laptop to the conference.
2. This college doesn't **allow smoking** on campus.
3. Kai **avoids drinking** alcohol.
4. Noah **can't help looking** at his phone.

Exercise 27
Now it's your turn to practice.

Write your answers using the verb followed by a gerund pattern.

1. What is something you **dislike doing** at school or in the office?
2. What time did you **finish eating** dinner last night?
3. What are you doing these days that you will **keep doing** for the next few months?
4. What does your college or office **prohibit doing**?
5. What do you **regret doing** or **regret not doing** in the past year?

Verbs Followed by Infinitives

In this lesson, we're going to look at verbs followed by an infinitive. Here are some of the more common ones:

agree	intend	refuse
arrange	manage	tend
decide	need	wait
don't care	offer	want
expect	plan	
hope	promise	

Look at some examples:

1. Do you think he'll **agree to work** on Saturday?
2. Grayson **arranged to meet** his client at 9:00 a.m.
3. Have you **decided to take** the job?
4. Isabella **intends to study** robotics in graduate school.

Some verbs can be followed by an object and then the infinitive. That object is usually a person. Here are some of the more common ones:

advise	hire	teach
ask	invite	tell
cause	order	warn
convince	permit	wish
enable	persuade	
encourage	remind	

Look at some examples:

1. I will **advise him to do** his internship during the spring semester.
2. Did you have a chance to **ask Luz to help** you with the project?
3. Ping told me that he **hired someone to work** in sales.
4. I'm so excited! They **invited me to run** a session at the workshop.

Write your answers using the verb followed by an infinitive pattern.

1. Imagine your classmate is having trouble deciding whether to take a job. What would you advise her to do?
2. During meetings, do you tend to speak up, or are you quieter?
3. Complete this sentence and explain why: "I would refuse to . . ."
4. When was the last time you taught someone how to do something?
5. What have you decided to do for your next vacation?

Verbs Followed by Either Gerunds or Infinitives

As we learned, verbs such as *like, prefer,* and *love* can be followed by either a gerund or an infinitive with no difference in meaning. There are five verbs—*stop, try, remember, forget,* and *regret*—that have a different meaning depending on whether they are followed by a gerund or an infinitive.

When you use **stop to do something**, it means "take a break to do something."

1. She **stopped to smoke**.
2. I **stopped to buy** coffee on the way to the office.

When you use **stop doing something**, it means "quit" or "finish."

1. I **stopped smoking** when I was in my mid-twenties. (I quit smoking.)
2. I **stopped buying** coffee on the way to the office. (I don't buy coffee anymore.)

When you **try to do something**, it means you are attempting to do something new or challenging.

1. I'm **trying to find** the best way to cook that soup.
2. Luca is **trying to learn** Portuguese.

When you **try doing something**, you're testing to see what happens.

1. I have an old laptop. I **tried turning** it on, but it didn't work. So I **tried using** a different AC adapter, but it still didn't work.
2. I **tried sending** Mia a few text messages, but she didn't reply. I'm going to **try calling** her.

When you **remember to do something**, it means, "It's my responsibility to do that."

1. I have to **remember to lock** my office.
2. Please **remember to wash** your hands before eating.

When you **remember doing something**, it means, "I did it and I have a memory of it."

1. I **remember going** to Istanbul. It was a great trip.
2. I **remember meeting** Elijah at the party. He was so funny.

When you **forget to do something**, it means, "I did not remember to do something important."

1. I **forgot to call** my grandmother on her birthday, and she was very upset.
2. The boss was angry because Oliver **forgot to ask** his customer to sign the contract.

When you **forget doing something**, it means, "I did it, but I don't remember doing it."

1. I **forgot paying** the telephone bill, so I mistakenly paid twice.
2. I **forgot meeting** Riley several years ago until she reminded me that we met in Chicago.

When you **regret to do something**, the meaning is "I'm sorry, but I must do this." We use this pattern to inform someone of bad news, using phrases like **I regret to tell you**, **I regret to say this**, and **I regret to have to do this**.

1. I **regret to tell** you that the company won't be giving a bonus this year.
2. I **regret to** have to do this, but I must inform you that your employment with our company has been terminated.

When you **regret doing something**, the meaning is "I did something that I regret."

1. I **regret lending** Mason my car. He returned it without any gasoline.
2. Mohammad said he **regrets asking** that girl for a date. He didn't know she had a boyfriend.

Exercise 29
Now it's your turn to practice.

Decide whether the sentences are correct.

1. On the way to my office this morning, I stopped smoking.
2. I regret going to that party last night. I am so tired today.
3. The phone isn't working? Have you tried to plug it in?
4. I forgot to close the window and now it's raining.

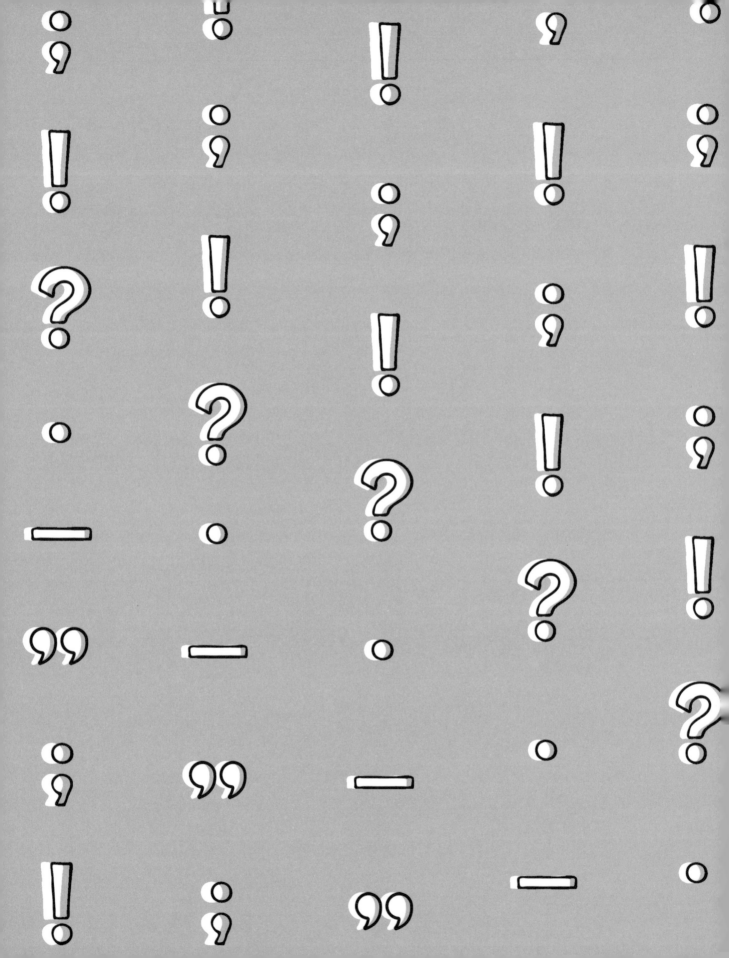

Chapter Five

Verb Tenses

Verb tenses are at the heart of the English language. At the basic level, verb tenses indicate time, and English has verb tenses that indicate past, present, and future time. This chapter will take us through the different kinds and when they're used.

The Three Forms of the Verb

English verbs have three forms: the base verb, the past verb, and the past participle.

The **base** form of the verb, also known as the infinitive form, can be used with or without *to*.

1. We always **work** from nine to five.
2. Please **check** the document before sending it.
3. I like **to hike** on this trail.
4. We need **to estimate** the cost for the customer.

There are two types of past verbs. Regular verbs have a past tense that ends in *-ed* according to the following spelling rules:

1. To form the past of most verbs, just add *ed*.
   a) Lily **showed** me her diploma.
   b) My mom **cooked** a nice lasagna for my birthday dinner.
   c) Everyone **worked** hard to prepare for the exam.

2. When the verb ends in *e*, just add *d*.

   a) We **faced** a few problems during the negotiations.
   b) The business school **moved** in 1979.
   c) The company **leased** two vans this month.

3. When a one-syllable word ends in a consonant or when the last syllable of the verb ending in a consonant is stressed, double the final consonant and add *ed*.

   a) We **planned** a thorough audit for our client.
   b) The meeting was **slotted** for 10:00 a.m., but it was rescheduled for 2:00 p.m.
   c) They **transmitted** the fax at 4:03 p.m.

4. When the verb ends in a *y* preceded by a consonant, change the *y* to *i* and add *ed*.

   a) She **hurried** to finish the math test on time.
   b) I **tried** to phone Silvana, but she didn't answer.
   c) Leo **studied** for six months to pass the TOEFL.

5. When the verb ends in a *y* preceded by a vowel, add *ed*.

   a) She **sprayed** the paint all over the wall.
   b) We really **enjoyed** the movie.
   c) The water leak **destroyed** the floor in the dorm.

Some irregular verbs don't follow the same spelling rules in their past tense form (like *build*, *send*, and *sell*).

1. Haruto's grandfather **built** this business in 1952.
2. Ella **sent** her first draft to the instructor.
3. So far, we have **sold** almost two thousand of these bags.

Exercise 30
Now it's your turn to practice.

Choose the correct form of the verb.

1. I always (listen / to listen / listened) to the radio in the car on the way to work.
2. I (go / went / gone) to Stockholm in 2017.
3. They usually (spend / to spend / spent) a lot of time in the office on the weekends.
4. We (buy / to buy / bought) a new car last month.
5. Can you (help / to help / helped) me with my project?

Simple Present

We use the **simple present** verb when we indicate usual true situations and facts.

1. Mouad **works** in the accounting department.
2. Water **freezes** at 32 degrees Fahrenheit.

However, the form of the verb changes depending on the subject of the sentence. When the subject is the third person (*he*, *she*, and *it*), the spelling of the verb changes.

I / you / we / they		she / he / it	
ask	make	asks	makes
become	need	becomes	needs
cook	practice	cooks	practices
do	study	does	studies
find	think	finds	thinks
get	use	gets	uses
know	want	knows	wants

The spelling rules that we covered (on page 6) apply to verbs as well. However, the spelling rules for *be* and *have* are irregular.

When the subject is *I*, use *am* or *have*.

When the subject is *you*, *we*, or *they*, use *are* or *have*.

When the subject is *she*, *he*, or *it*, use *is* or *has*.

Exercise 31
Now it's your turn to practice.

Write the correct form of the verb.

1. We _____ to finish this project by Friday. (need)
2. The professor _____ us to work in groups. (want)
3. I really _____ I have to cut down on drinking coffee. (think)
4. She has a high GPA because she _____ hard. (study)
5. You _____ very well. Did you learn from your grandmother? (cook)

Simple Past

We use the **simple past** tense to indicate completed actions. We generally use the simple past with phrases or in a context that indicates a single point in the past.
    Four spelling rules relate to regular verbs.

1. When the verb ends in *e*, just add *d*.

bake**d**	dine**d**	perceive**d**
calculate**d**	grate**d**	worke**d**
debate**d**	hope**d**	

2. When the verb ends in a stressed vowel and consonant combination, double the consonant and add *ed*.

beg…beg**ged**	pin…pin**ned**	sob…sob**bed**
flip…flip**ped**	rip…rip**ped**	stop…stop**ped**
jog…jog**ged**	shop…shop**ped**	

3. When the verb ends in a consonant followed by *y*, change the *y* to *i* and add *ed*.

apply…appl**ied**	comply…compl**ied**	try…tr**ied**
bully…bull**ied**	imply…impl**ied**	unify…unif**ied**
cry…cr**ied**	rely…rel**ied**	

4. For all other regular verbs, just add *ed*.

accept…accept**ed**	employ…employ**ed**	research…research**ed**
crush…crush**ed**	offend…offend**ed**	sail…sail**ed**
deploy…deploy**ed**	relay…relay**ed**	

Here are some examples using the simple past form of regular verbs:

1. Jacob **worked** in Panama for two years.
2. Did you know that last week Luna **applied** to the position in Barcelona?
3. I **relayed** the information about your expense report to the boss.

English also has many irregular verbs with a unique past tense spelling. Here are a few:

begin…began	cost…cost	pay…paid
bid…bid	hold…held	teach…taught
build…built	mistake…mistook	

Here are some examples using the simple past form of irregular verbs:

1. When we **held** a lunch meeting at the steakhouse, it **cost** about $75 a person.
2. We **bid** on several contracts this month.
3. I heard that this instructor has **taught** English in Japan.

> ## Exercise 32
> ## Now it's your turn to practice.

Choose the correct form of the past verb in each sentence.

1. I heard Emily .... the boss to let us go home early on Friday. (persuade)
2. The only way we can improve profits is to .... costs. (cut)
3. The reason you .... points on the essay is that you forgot to write the conclusion. (lose)
4. The professor .... a field trip to ABC Labs. (organize)
5. Have you .... the problem with the e-mail server? (identify)

Simple Future

There are a few ways in English to indicate the future, depending on whether we are referring to set plans, predictions, or schedules.

We use a form of *be going to* followed by a base verb to indicate a set plan, an appointment, etc.

1. A friend of mine **is going to** get married this weekend.
2. I **am going to** go to the beach on Sunday.
3. Rhona **is going to** see a movie tonight.

We can also use the present progressive tense for the future when we talk about something we have already made plans or arranged to do.

1. A friend of mine **is getting** married this weekend.
2. I **am going** to the beach this weekend.
3. Maya **is seeing** a movie tonight.

We use *will* followed by a base verb to make a prediction or guess or when there is not a set plan.

1. Someday, I **will** find true love.
2. I think I **will** move to Florida when I retire.
3. I'm sure the vacation **will** be a lot of fun.

We use the simple present tense for the future to indicate schedules and events in the future that have a set starting or ending time.

1. The workshop **begins** at 9:00 p.m.
2. Check-in at the hotel **starts** at 1:00 p.m.
3. The flight to Zurich **departs** at noon.

Exercise 33
Now it's your turn to practice.

Answer the following questions using the proper form of the simple future.

1. Write one or two sentences about your plans for tomorrow.
2. Write one or two sentences about your plans for the weekend.
3. Make a prediction about the weather tomorrow or the day after tomorrow.
4. What time does school or work start in the morning?

Present Perfect

The **present perfect** tense is formed with *have* followed by the past participle form of the verb. For example, *I have eaten, she has eaten, we have eaten*, etc.

We use the present perfect to indicate experience before and up to the present time.

1. I **have been** to Thailand several times.
2. Dr. Thompson **has helped** many students prepare their graduate thesis.
3. You guys did a great job. We **have never sold** that many widgets before.

We also use the present perfect to connect the past to the present time. You can use the present perfect with "since" to connect one point in the past to now.

1. Josiah **has been** on the faculty here **since** 1985.
2. I **have wanted** to take a trip to NASA **since** I was a little kid.
3. Our company **has worked** with this ad agency **since** it opened.

You can use the present perfect with *for* to connect a period of time in the past to now.

1. I was surprised to learn that Adalyn **has lived** in Pasadena **for** more than fifty years.
2. This factory **has been** open **for** ninety-five years.
3. We **have worked** on this experiment **for** a number of months and **have** finally **made** a breakthrough in the lab.

Exercise 34
Now it's your turn to practice.

Decide if the present perfect is used correctly. Correct any errors.

1. I have been to that store many times.
2. We know that agent very well. We have visited her last month.
3. Marco's family business has sold pasta for three generations.
4. Nora has been a student in this school last semester, too.
5. I'm not sure if I have seen Brian this week or not.

Past Perfect

The **past perfect** tense is formed with *had* and the past participle form of the verb. For example, *I had worked, he had known, she had told,* etc.

   We use the past perfect to indicate the earlier of two events that happened in the past.

1. By the time we arrived, they **had** already **finished** the first course.
2. Luckily it **had stopped** snowing when I got to the office.
3. Ellie **had learned** programming on her own before she started college.

   We also use the past perfect to indicate experience before and up to a point in past time.

1. I **had worked** in Japan before coming to this office in Dallas.
2. Do you know if Jayce **had had** any sales experience before getting the job?
3. I wish I **had known** it was Maffi's birthday.

Exercise 35
Now it's your turn to practice.

Answer the questions using the past perfect tense.

1. How long had you studied English before you got this book?
2. Are you in school now? Had you ever attended a language school before this one?
3. Had you ever studied the past perfect tense before getting this book?
4. Had you thought grammar was difficult before using this book?
5. Think of what you studied in your last English class. Had you studied that same topic before?

Future Perfect

The **future perfect** tense is formed with *will have* and the past participle form of the verb. For example, *I will have gone, he will have finished, she will have studied,* etc.

   We use the future perfect to indicate that an event will finish by a particular time in the future.

1. We are going to the dinner party after work, so by the time we arrive at the restaurant, they **will have finished** the first course.
2. By the time Ivan starts college, his older sister **will have graduated**.
3. Giancarlo **will have completed** his internship by the start of summer vacation.

Exercise 36
Now it's your turn to practice.

Answer the questions using the future perfect tense.

1. What will you have done or accomplished by noon tomorrow?
2. What will you have done by next month?
3. What will you have done by next year?
4. What will you have done by the time you turn five years older than you are now?
5. What will you have done by the time you retire?

Present Progressive

The **present progressive** tense is formed with the *be* verb (*am, is, are*) and the *ing* form of the verb. For example, *I am driving, she is living, he is cooking,* etc.

We use the present progressive tense to indicate actions that are happening right now. This tense usually refers to temporary situations.

1. Hi, Daniel. I'm glad you can join us. We **are talking** about the main characters in Macbeth.
2. I **am listening** to you, but I'm not sure what you are talking about.
3. What **are** you **looking** for? I **am trying** to find my keys.

We also use the present progressive tense with phrases like *these days, this week,* etc., to indicate actions that are happening around this time.

1. The new guy in my office **is staying** in a temporary apartment this month.
2. I **am studying** with a really interesting grammar book these days.
3. It's almost the end of the semester, so everyone **is working** on their term papers.

We can also use the present progressive tense to indicate the future, especially when the future event is a set plan.

1. The CEO **is arriving** on Tuesday, and Julian **is picking** her up at the airport.
2. We **are having** dinner at a very nice Persian restaurant after the meeting.
3. I've made my decision. I **am going** to business school to get an MBA.

Exercise 37
Now it's your turn to practice.

Decide whether the present progressive is used correctly. Correct any errors.

1. Wyatt is going to call on some customers in Chicago next week.
2. Can you turn down the music? I'm studying for a psychology exam.
3. Abby said she is working out at that new gym in Brooklyn.
4. The sales meeting is starting every Friday at noon.
5. I'm really excited because I'm leaving for my trip.

Past Progressive

The **present progressive** tense is formed with the past form of the *be* verb and the *ing* form of the verb. For example, *I was working, she was singing, we were traveling,* etc.

We use the past progressive to indicate that some action was happening at a particular time in the past. Like the present progressive, the past progressive refers to temporary situations.

1. I **was traveling** in Europe last summer.
2. I **was binge-watching** *The Big Bang Theory* with Henri yesterday.
3. I **was working** in the lab when she called.

We use the past progressive with the simple past to indicate that one event happened while the other action was going on. In this way, the past progressive sets the background scene for the other action.

1. While I **was eating** dinner, somebody rang the doorbell.
2. As I **was leaving** the house, I saw a huge black crow on my car.
3. A car hit a pole and the power went out while I **was recording** a podcast.

We use the past progressive with words like *always, constantly, usually,* etc., when we want to mention typical actions in the past.

1. In the summertime, my grandfather **was** always **watching** baseball on TV.
2. Oh, I remember Seoyun. She **was** constantly **telling** jokes in the office.
3. Every time I looked at Beth, she **was staring** at her smartphone.

Exercise 38
Now it's your turn to practice.

Answer the questions using the past progressive tense.

1. What were you doing thirty minutes ago?
2. What was the last project you were working on?
3. What music were you listening to last night?
4. Where were you living five years ago?
5. Think about a relative you were close with as a child. What were they always doing that you enjoyed?

Future Progressive

The **future progressive** tense is formed with the future form of the *be* verb and the *ing* form of the verb. For example, *I will be cooking, she is going to be working, we will be leaving,* etc.

We use the future progressive to indicate that some action will be happening at a particular time in the future. Like the present progressive, the future progressive refers to temporary situations.

1. By this time tomorrow, we **will be flying** to the Caribbean.
2. In less than a week, we**'ll be getting** married.
3. I**'m going to be leaving** the office at 4:00 p.m. today for an appointment.

We can also use the future progressive with the simple present and words like *before, after,* and *when.*

1. The baby **will be sleeping** when we arrive, so let's keep our voices down.
2. I heard that the IT people **are going to be working** on the server tonight.
3. I**'ll be studying** way before finals week starts, that's for sure.

Answer the questions using the future progressive tense.

1. What will you be doing in an hour from now?
2. What will you be doing tomorrow morning at 9:00 a.m.?
3. Where do you think you'll be living in five years?
4. Think about your boss or professor. When do you think that person will be retiring?
5. When do you think you will be finishing studying the lessons in this book?

Present Perfect Progressive

The **present perfect progressive** is formed with *have/has been* followed by the *ing* form of the verb. For example, *I have been working, she has been studying, it has been raining,* etc.

We use the present perfect progressive to indicate actions and situations that started in the past and are continuing now.

1. We **have been negotiating** with that vendor for a few months, and I think we've finally come up with a win-win deal.
2. I **have been working on** my team's performance evaluations for a few weeks. I am going to submit them to HR tomorrow.
3. It **has been snowing** all night. We are going to have trouble getting to the office this morning.

Generally, the focus of the present perfect progressive is how people spend their time.

1. You**'ve been working** on that report for a few hours. Why don't you take a break?
2. Arianna **has been dealing** with that account since 2014. I've got big shoes to fill.
3. I haven't seen you since you transferred to the planning department. What **have you been doing** lately?

We also use the present perfect progressive when we talk about actions that have just finished and have a connection to something now.

1. Sorry to have kept you waiting. Have you **been waiting** long?
2. Have you **been crying**? Your eyes are red.
3. I've **been trying** to clear a paper jam, so now my hands are covered in toner.

Exercise 40
Now it's your turn to practice.

Imagine you are working as an intern in a science lab. Respond to the questions using the present perfect progressive and a little imagination.

1. Why are there reference books all over the lab table?
2. Are you still taking notes?
3. How long have you been looking at those beakers?
4. Why has the boss's door been closed all day?
5. What have you been doing in the lab all night?

Past Perfect Progressive

The **past perfect progressive** tense is formed with *had been* followed by the *ing* form of the verb. For example, *I had been studying, she had been writing, it had been snowing,* etc.

We use the past perfect progressive to indicate actions and situations that started in the past and continued to or ended at a particular point in the past.

1. I remember when I learned of my promotion. I **had been working** in the sales office at that time.
2. Gabriel **had been studying** economics before he changed his major to accounting.
3. The undergraduate students **had been living** in off-campus housing until the college built these dorms.

We use the past perfect progressive with *for* and *since* to indicate how long something had been going on until a particular point in the past.

1. We **had been working** in the conference room *for* about four hours when the computer network went down.
2. William **had been studying** Korean *since* he was in middle school and only stopped about a year ago.

The past perfect progressive is used to emphasize continuing activities and situations, whereas the past perfect just indicates completed actions.

1. I **had been working** all day without a break, and I suddenly got hungry.
2. I **had worked** all day yesterday without a break and decided to leave the office.

```
Exercise 41
Now it's your turn to practice.
```

Complete the sentences using the past perfect progressive and a little imagination.

1. The accounting manager was fired because _____ .
2. A guy walked into me on the sidewalk because _____ .
3. Madelyn passed all of her final exams because _____ .
4. Isaac fell down at the office holiday party because _____ .
5. I was able to _____ because _____ .

Future Perfect Progressive

The **future perfect progressive** is formed with *will have been* followed by the *ing* form of the verb. For example, *I will have been working, she will have been studying, we will have been living,* etc.

We use the future perfect progressive to indicate actions and situations that will continue until a particular point in time in the future. We use this tense to launch ourselves into the future and look back at the entire duration of the action or situation.

1. By the time I am fifty years old, I **will have been working** for thirty-two years.
2. We started working on this budget at noon. If we continue until midnight, we **will have been working** for twelve hours.
3. When you begin your medical residency, you **will have been studying** medicine for eight years.

```
Exercise 42
Now it's your turn to practice.
```

Complete the sentences using the future perfect progressive.

1. By this time tomorrow, _____ .
2. By my next birthday, _____ .
3. By this time next week, _____ .
4. By the time I finish all of the lessons in this book, _____ .
5. By the time I retire, _____ .

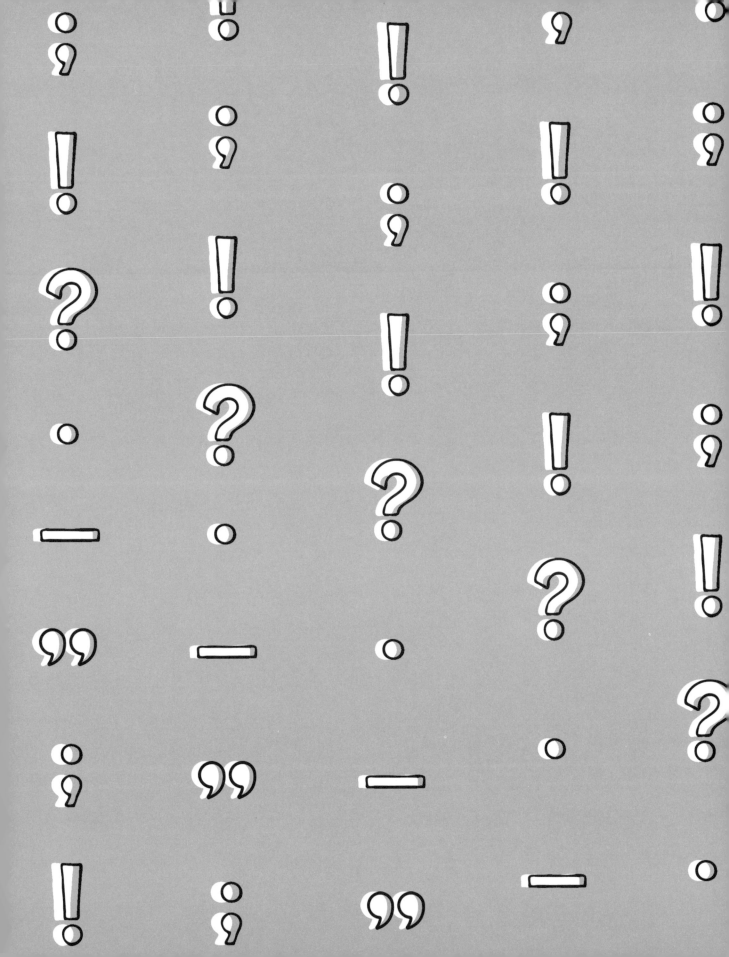

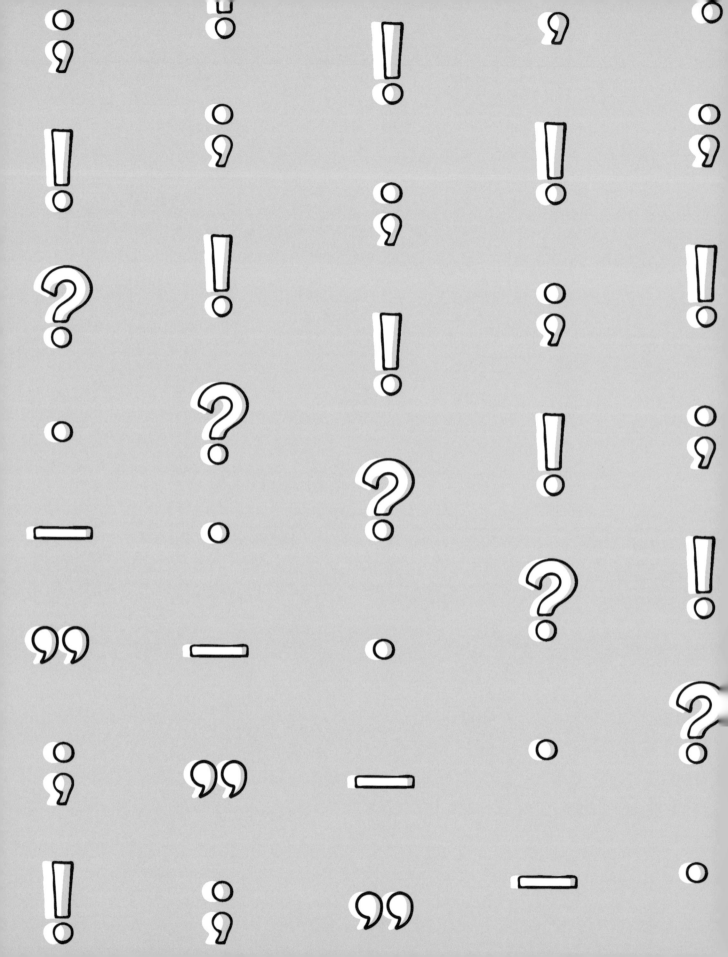

Chapter Six

Advanced Ideas with Verbs

In this chapter, we'll look at modal verbs, causatives, and conditionals. Knowing these patterns will help you express a variety of ideas with verbs beyond verb tenses. The topics here also come up on those standardized English exams, so it's helpful to understand and be able to use them.

Modal Verbs

Modal verbs are used in combination with other verbs to indicate ability, permission, possibility, or obligation. In many cases, like *must* or *should*, a modal verb can have a variety of meanings and uses.

Modals Part 1: *Must / Have to / Need to*

Must shows necessity. We usually use **must** when someone makes a rule or law. When you **must** do something, there is no choice.

1. When you travel abroad, you **must** have a passport.
2. You **must** stop at a red light.
3. You **must** speak quietly in the library.

The negative form of **must** is **must not**. However, the meaning of **must not** is prohibition (in other words, **must not** means **don't do that**).

1. You **must not** smoke here.
2. You **must not** pass a red light without stopping.
3. You **must not** shout in the library.

Have to is like **must**. **Have to** shows necessity, and we use **have to** when someone makes a rule or law that we need to follow. **Have to** is softer than *must*, but like *must*, there is no choice.

1. When you travel abroad, you **have to** have a passport.
2. You **have to** stop at a red light.
3. You **have to** speak quietly in the library.

In a negative sentence, **don't have to** is used to talk about what is not necessary. There is no negative form of **must**, so we do not use **don't must**.

1. When you travel from Baltimore to Phoenix, you **don't have to** bring a passport.
2. You **don't have to** stop at a green light.
3. You **don't have to** speak quietly in the library café.

Had to is used to talk about past necessity. There is no past form of *must* to mean necessity.

1. When I traveled abroad, I **had to** have a passport.
2. You **had to** stop at the red light. That's why the police stopped you.
3. You **have to** speak quietly in the library. That's why the librarian scolded us.

Like **must** and **have to**, **need to** is also used to talk about what is necessary. The basic difference between the term **need to** and the terms **must** and **have to** is where the necessity comes from. Generally, with **must** and **have to**, the necessity comes from someone other than ourselves. With **need to**, the necessity comes from ourselves. Compare the following examples:

1. When you travel abroad, you **must** have a passport. *The necessity comes from the law.*
2. You **have to** be quiet in the library. *The necessity comes from a rule.*
3. I **need to** go on a diet. *The necessity comes from myself.*

Need to can be used when you (or someone else) make the rules or plan for yourself.

1. I **need to** exercise more.
2. Matt said he **needs to** get a new computer.
3. We **need to** leave by 5:00 p.m. to get to the station on time.

Exercise 43
Now it's your turn to practice.

Complete the questions or statements using a form of *must, have to,* or *need to.*

1. My flight is at 7:00 a.m. tomorrow, so I .... wake up at 4:00 a.m.
2. When you have a job interview, you .... be late.
3. Paisley is lucky. Even though she is the store manager, she .... work on weekends.
4. The boss said the marketing plan we submitted looked okay, so we .... make any changes.
5. I think I .... start looking for a new job. This company isn't doing well.

Modals Part 2: *Had Better / Should / Ought to*

Had better is used when we give someone a warning. **Had better** means that if you don't do it, something bad will happen.

1. It's very cold outside today. You **had better** dry your hair before going out.
2. You still have that headache? You **had better** see a doctor.
3. If you want to pass this course, you **had better** do all of your homework.

Should and **ought to** are used to talk about something that is "a good idea" and are often used to make a suggestion. You can use either term in any of these examples:

1. We **should** go home now. It's getting late.
2. You **ought to** let the boss look that over before you e-mail it.
3. When you come to NYC, you **should** go to Central Park.

We also use **should** and **ought to** when we talk about situations that are probably going to happen because they are usual and expected.

1. Class **should** be finished by 1:00 p.m. *Class usually finishes at 1:00 p.m.*
2. Milena **ought to** be here soon. She left her house 30 minutes ago. *It takes 30 minutes to get here.*

We use **should have** followed by the **past participle verb** when we talk about a situation that we expected to happen in the past but that did not happen. We also use this form to talk about past regrets. We don't use **ought to** in these situations.

1. The train **should have gotten** here 10 minutes ago. *I expected the train to be here 10 minutes ago.*
2. I **should have studied** harder in school. *I regret not studying harder in school.*

Exercise 44
Now it's your turn to practice.

Complete the statements using *had better* or *should/ought to*.

1. The sales rep _____ be here soon. He is usually on time.
2. This meeting schedule looks fine to me, but I think we _____ have Elena look it over before we send it out.
3. The doctor told David that he _____ stop smoking.
4. I think you _____ go back and make sure you locked the door.
5. I think I _____ start exercising. I need to lose a little weight.

Modals Part 3: *May / Might / Can*

In many cases, we use **may** and **might** with the same meaning.
We use **may** and **might** to show that something is possible.

1. It **may** rain tomorrow (or) It **might** rain tomorrow.
2. I **may** come to the office this weekend (or) I **might** come to the office this weekend.
3. Insook **may** visit us at the trade show (or) Insook **might** visit us at the trade show.

In formal situations, we use **may**, not **might**, when we express our wishes or hopes. This is typically used more in written than spoken English.

1. **May** you have a very successful trip.
2. Congratulations on your wedding. **May** you have a lifetime of happiness and joy.

We use **may**, not **might**, to politely ask for something or for permission.

1. **May** I have another cup of coffee?
2. **May** I ask you a question?

We use **can** to talk about ability that comes after a certain amount of practice or study.

1. Lila **can** use InDesign, so I think we should have her work on the brochure.
2. Angelo **can** type faster than anyone else in the office.
3. Let me know if you need any help at the conference. I **can** speak Japanese.
4. Katia **can** tell you anything about history.

We use **can** to talk about having the opportunity to do something.

1. By working in the marketing department, you **can** experience so many things.
2. In a university, you **can** meet many students from various countries.
3. You **can** find all kinds of publications in the main library.

We use **can** to express permission.

1. You **can** leave the office as soon as you finish that paperwork.
2. I **can** dress as I like for work.
3. The manager said we **can** go home early.

We use **can** to make requests.

1. **Can** you help me with my term paper?
2. **Can** I turn down the air conditioner?
3. **Can** we take a break from studying?

We use **can** to make a suggestion or offer.

1. We **can** take a break now if you'd like.
2. What do you want for lunch? We **can** have pizza or burgers.
3. Asher has to leave early, so he **can** do his presentation first.

We use **can** to talk about usual or typical situations.

1. Working long hours **can** be dangerous for your health.
2. Be careful of that dog. He **can** be aggressive.
3. Bosses and teachers **can** be demanding.

Exercise 45
Now it's your turn to practice.

Complete the statements using *may*, *might*, or *can*.

1. I haven't finished my work, so I _____ stay here a bit longer.
2. Why don't you ask Cameron to help you? He _____ use all of the software.
3. Nicolas is a nice guy, but sometimes he _____ talk forever.
4. Grace wasn't feeling well, so she _____ not come to work today.
5. Some questions on the TOEFL _____ be tricky, so read them carefully.

Modals Part 4: *Could*

We use **could** as the past tense of **can** in a negative sentence describing ability.

1. I **couldn't** use Excel before I started working here.
2. Lincoln **couldn't** find his wallet this morning.
3. Because of the heavy traffic, we **couldn't** catch the flight.

We don't use **could** as the past tense of **can** in a positive sentence describing ability. When we talk about **ability** in a positive sentence in the past, we prefer to use **was able to** instead of *could*.

1. I **was able to** find the jacket I was looking for.
2. We **were able to** get on the next flight.
3. Finally, Ezra **was able to** find his keys.

We use **could** to indicate possibility or that something is likely to happen.

1. They **could** be right. This contract is complicated, so we should have the legal department look at it.
2. I would go if I **could** afford it.
3. This shelf was not installed properly. I think it **could** easily fall.

We use **could** to make polite requests.

1. **Could** we use the phone?
2. **Could** I borrow your calculator?

We use **could** followed by the past particle verb to indicate annoyance because of something that has not been done. The *if condition* is often unstated and implied.

1. We **could have gotten** an earlier flight if they had told us about it.
2. They **could have told** me that they were coming late!

We use **could** to indicate a person's strong inclination to do something or behave in a certain way.

1. He irritates me so much that I **could** scream.
2. She **could** be so negative sometimes.

Exercise 46
Now it's your turn to practice.

Answer the questions in full sentences using *could* or *be able to*.

1. What is something you couldn't do two years ago?
2. Were you able to keep your GPA above 3.5 last semester?
3. Do you think it could snow within the next seven days?
4. Do you think an AI robot could replace you at work?
5. Is there anything you could have done differently over the past year?

Causatives

We use **causative verbs** to indicate that a person or a thing causes something to happen. The most common causative verbs are **make**, **let**, **have**, and **get**.

When we use the causative form of **make**, **let**, **have**, and **get** and the object of those verbs is performing the action, we **use the base form of the main verb**. Someone causes someone to do something.

In its causative form, **make** has the meaning of "force." We use **make** followed by a *person* followed by a **base verb.**

1. The boss **made** *Jermaine* **work** on the report all day.
2. The professor **makes** *his students* **write** a journal every day.
3. Jenny **makes** *her son* **eat** all of his vegetables.

In its causative form, **let** has the meaning of "permit." We use **let** followed by a *person* followed by a **base verb.**

1. My manager **lets** *us* **go** home early if we've finished our work.
2. Connor **let** *me* **use** his tablet in the library.
3. The airline **let** *Tia* **switch** her flight without a penalty.

Have, in its causative form, has the meaning of "ask" or "arrange." We use **have** followed by a *person* followed by a **base verb.**

1. The boss **had** *Juan* **work** on the meeting schedule.
2. Callie **had** *the IT department* **repair** her laptop.
3. Emery **had** *her students* **decorate** the classroom for the holidays.

In its causative form, **get** has the meaning of "persuade." We use **get** followed by a *person* followed by an **infinitive**.

1. The boss **got** *Lorenzo* **to play** golf on Sunday.
2. I **got** *him* **to agree** to help me paint the house.
3. We **got** *Colton* **to join** our carpool in the morning.

We also use the causative of **have** and **get** when we ask someone to do a job for us. We use **have** or **get** followed by a *thing* followed by a **past participle verb**. You can have something done or you can get something done.

1. I **had** *my hair* **cut**.
2. I need **to have** *my car* **serviced**.
3. I **had** *my house* **painted** last month.

> **Exercise 47**
> **Now it's your turn to practice.**

Answer the questions using the causative form of **make**, **let**, **have**, and **get**.

1. What time does your employer make you start work in the morning?
2. Imagine you are the boss of a small IT office. What would you let your staff do (or not let them do)?
3. When was the last time a classmate or coworker had you do something for them?
4. Would it be easy for a friend to get you to wake up at 5:00 a.m. to go hiking?
5. What is something that you want to have done around the house?

Conditionals

We use the **conditional** form to indicate that an action or situation will have a particular result. There are four types of conditional sentences, and each of them uses *if* to introduce the condition.

Zero Conditional

We use this to talk about usual true situations and facts. The structure is **if . . . present tense verb . . . present tense verb**.

1. **If** the temperature **reaches** 100 degrees Celsius, water **boils**.
2. **If** it **snows**, driving **becomes** dangerous.
3. **If** you **come** to work late, your pay **gets** docked.

First Conditional

We use this to talk about things that will, can, or may happen in the future and/or probable results in the future. The structure is **if, present tense verb, future tense verb (will, be going to, can, may, might)**.

1. **If** it **snows** tomorrow, I **will not drive** my car.
2. **If** I **am** late for work again, the boss **is going to be** angry.
3. **If** I **need** help, I **might call** you.

Second Conditional

We use this to talk about imaginary and hypothetical situations. The structure is **if, past tense verb (would, could, might, may)** followed by a **base verb**.

1. **If** I **won** the lottery, I **would buy** a big yacht.
2. **If** I ***were** taller, I **could be** a better basketball player.
3. **If** Tom **were** here, he **would be able to** fix the computer.

   *We use **were** in the second conditional, regardless of the subject.

Depending on the situation or the context, sometimes we can use either the first or second conditional.

1. **If** I **win** the lottery, I **will buy** a big yacht.
2. **If** I **won** the lottery, I **would buy** a big yacht.

But sometimes, again depending on the situation or the context, we can't.

1. **If** I **am** taller, I **can be** a better basketball player. *A child could say this, but not an adult, because being taller is not possible for an adult.*
2. **If** I **were** taller, I **could be** a better basketball player.

We often use the second conditional phrase **If I were you** to give advice.

1. **If I were you**, I **would not eat** junk food.
2. Are you having car trouble? **If I were you,** I **would take** the car back to the dealer.
3. Akeno's wife is mad at him. **If I were Akeno**, I **would bring** her some roses and apologize.

Third Conditional

We use this to talk about imaginary and hypothetical situations in the past. It is often used to talk about how the past might have been different.

The pattern is **if, past perfect tense, would/could/might/may, have, past participle verb**.

1. **If** I **had known** about the exam, I **would have studied.**
2. **If** I **had won** the lottery, I **would have bought** a big yacht.
3. **If** I **had seen** you at the mall, I **would have said** hello.

Exercise 48
Now it's your turn to practice.

Decide whether the conditional form is used correctly. Correct any errors.

1. If the temperature drops below 32 degrees Fahrenheit, water will freeze.
2. If you have any trouble with your term paper, let me know and I will help you.
3. I would have gone to the meeting if I knew about it.
4. If they will not sign the contract, we will schedule another meeting with them.
5. If Violet were here, she would be able to help us out.

Chapter Seven

Prepositions

Prepositions are words such as *at*, *on*, and *to* that show the relationship between the noun and the other words in a sentence. We'll explore some prepositions and the different ways they can be used.

Prepositions of Time

We use *at, in*, and *on* to indicate time. *At* is for clock time, and *on* is for a day or date. For all other longer periods of time, like months, seasons, years, centuries, etc., use *in*.

Clock time	Days and dates	Longer periods of time
at three o'clock	**on** Sunday	**in** May
at 10:30 a.m.	**on** Tuesdays	**in** summer
at noon	**on** March 6	**in** 2010
at night	**on** June 25, 2020	**in** the 1990s
at bedtime	**on** Christmas Day	**in** the eighteenth century
at sunrise	**on** my birthday	**in** the Ice Age

Here are some examples:

1. I have a meeting **at** 9:00 a.m.
2. Cala is going to give an HR presentation **on** Friday.
3. This company always gives you a day off **on** your birthday.
4. I suggest you visit Paris **in** the spring.
5. That type of music was popular **in** the early eighteenth century.

We also have some set phrases with the prepositions *in, at, on*, and *during*, which we use to indicate time. These are *in the morning, in the afternoon, in the evening, at night, during the week*, and *on the weekend*.

1. We are having a marketing meeting **in** the morning.
2. I don't have any classes **in** the afternoon.
3. Aisha's flight arrives **in** the evening.
4. Half of the call center staff works **at** night.
5. I work hard **during** the week.

When we say *last, next, every*, and *this*, we do not add *at, in*, or *on*.

1. I saw Ming **last** week.
2. Jamal is coming back **next** Tuesday.
3. We go skiing **every** winter.
4. We'll call you **this** evening.

> **Exercise 49**
> **Now it's your turn to practice.**

Fill in the blanks with the correct preposition.

1. The final exam begins _____ 4:00 p.m.
2. The next team meeting is _____ June 3.
3. The nursing course is only held _____ the spring semester.
4. I can't believe the boss is making us work _____ the weekend.
5. Charlotte became the office manager _____ 2002.
6. There's not much traffic _____ night.

Prepositions of Location

We often use *at* and *in* to indicate position or location in general. Both of these sentences tell us about Mila's location.

1. Mila is **at** her office.
2. Mila is **in** her office.

When we speak in a general way, we can use either *at* or *in* to describe the location. However, both *at* and *in* have some specific uses and meanings.

When we use *at* to indicate a location, it refers to the action that usually happens at that location. Notice also in these examples that the verb is an action verb:

1. I bought this shirt on sale **at** the department store.
2. Mateo had a coffee **at** a nice café.
3. Let's study **at** the library.

When we use *in* to indicate a location, it simply refers to the location itself and not any particular action. Notice also in these examples that the verb is the *be* verb:

1. I was **in** the department store yesterday.
2. Mateo is **in** a café on Madison Ave.
3. We have been **in** the library for three hours. Let's go home.

Some set phrases with *at* and *in* have a specific meaning.

1. Jayden is **in the hospital**. *He is a patient there.*
2. I was **at work** all night last night. *I was working in my office.*
3. Rishima is **at college**, so her sister has their bedroom to herself. *Rishima is living at college.*

We use *in* when we indicate a place with a border, like **in** a country, **in** a city, **in** a town, **in** a county, and **in** a neighborhood.

1. Jill lives **in** France.
2. Ethan spent a week **in** London on business.
3. Samir lives **in** Brooklyn, but he works **in** Manhattan.

We also use *in* when we indicate a place with walls or fences, like **in** a park, **in** a building, and **in** a box.

1. It's a nice day. Let's have a picnic **in** the park.
2. Her husband works **in** an Art Deco building.
3. We have a few bottles of wine **in** the refrigerator.

We use both *in* and *on* when we indicate directions (north, east, south, and west), but the grammar is different depending on how those direction words are used.
When north, east, south, and west are used as **nouns**, we use *in the*.

1. New York is **in the** East, and California **in the** West.
2. It's cold **in the** North, especially in the winter.
3. Some people **in the** South like to eat spicy foods.

But when north, east, south, and west are used as **adjectives**, we use *on the*.

1. Camilla lives **on the** west side of town.
2. There are many flags **on the** south wall of the building.
3. Sebastian's office is **on the** Upper West Side.

We use *at* when we indicate an address. An address contains a number and a street name.

1. His office is **at** 475 Ocean Avenue.
2. Eliana works **at** 500 Broadway.
3. I live **at** 333 Lombard Street.

We use *on* when we indicate a street name but not the address.

1. His office is **on** Ocean Avenue.
2. There are a lot of interesting places **on** Broadway.
3. There used to be many discount shops **on** Canal Street.

We also use *at* when we indicate a particular point on a street or in a town.

1. His office is **at** the corner of Ocean and 40th St.
2. I think James lives **at** the end of this block.

But we use *in* when we indicate the middle of something.

1. My office is **in** the middle of the block.
2. There is a lake **in** the middle of the park.

We also use *at* to indicate one specific point during a trip.

1. This train will stop **at** Lincoln Center, Times Square, and Soho.
2. I stopped **at** the coffee shop on the way to my office.

Exercise 50
Now it's your turn to practice.

Complete the sentence using *at, in,* or *on.*

1. Aliyah met her husband when she was working (at / in / on) Yahoo.
2. I was (at / in / on) work until 11:00 p.m. trying to finish the marketing project.
3. I didn't realize you were (at / in / on) the kitchen.
4. Scarlett lives (at / in / on) the south side of the city.
5. The speaker system is (at / in / on) the middle of the table.

Preposition Collocations

Collocations are words that occur together frequently. In this lesson, we're going to look at some of the most common ones that occur with prepositions and nouns, verbs, and adjectives.

Preposition Collocations with Nouns

approach to	experience in	reason for
attempt at	increase in	research into
cause of	investigation into	response to
change in	knowledge of	success in
difference in	need for	
example of	reaction to	

1. This company's **approach to** marketing is very impressive.
2. I like our new professor. She has great **knowledge of** robotics.
3. I am writing in **response to** your job posting.

Preposition Collocations with Verbs

apply for
associate with
belong to
comply with
concentrate on
contribute to

deal with
elaborate on
graduate from
inquire about
participate in

prepare for
search for
specialize in
succeed in
work for

1. To **apply for** this position, please submit your résumé.
2. Our firm **specializes in** immigration law.
3. I'd like to help you **prepare for** your dissertation.

Preposition Collocations with Adjectives

affiliated with
committed to
conscious of
experienced in
familiar with
grateful for

impressed by
inspired by
interested in
involved in
optimistic about

prepared for
responsible for
serious about
skilled in
successful in

1. Ryan's new company is **affiliated with** FIFA.
2. I am **grateful for** the opportunity to interview for this position.
3. As you can see by my résumé, I am **skilled in** all of the key areas.

Exercise 51
Now it's your turn to practice.

Reply to the questions using the collocation in your answer.

1. What is necessary for **success in** the twenty-first century?
2. What have you made an **attempt at** recently?
3. When was the last time you **participated in** a lecture or seminar?
4. How many foreign languages are you **familiar with**?
5. What have you been **impressed by** recently?

Phrasal Verbs

A **phrasal verb** is a verb and preposition combination used as an **idiom**, which is a phrase that has a unique meaning that is different from the meaning of individual words in the phrase. There are three key points to remember when using phrasal verbs.

1. **Transitive phrasal verbs** are followed by a direct object.
   a) It's a bit chilly outside. Why don't you **put on** a jacket?
   b) Can you please **turn on** the light?
   c) At 4:00 p.m. I have to **pick up** Chloe at the airport.
   d) We have to **put off** the meeting because the boss has to leave early today.

2. **Intransitive phrasal verbs** are not followed by a direct object.
   a) A good cup of coffee can certainly help me **wake up**.
   b) How did your research project **turn out**?
   c) Alexei **showed up** late for work and the boss was really upset.
   d) Retail sales usually **fall off** after the Christmas holiday season.

3. Some phrasal verbs are separable. This means that you can put the direct object between the verb and the preposition. If the direct object is a pronoun, it must come between the verb and the preposition, not after the preposition.
   a) Please **take off** your shoes.
   b) Please take **your** shoes **off**.
   c) Please **take** them **off**.

Exercise 52
Now it's your turn to practice.

Can you list ten phrasal verbs that were not mentioned here?

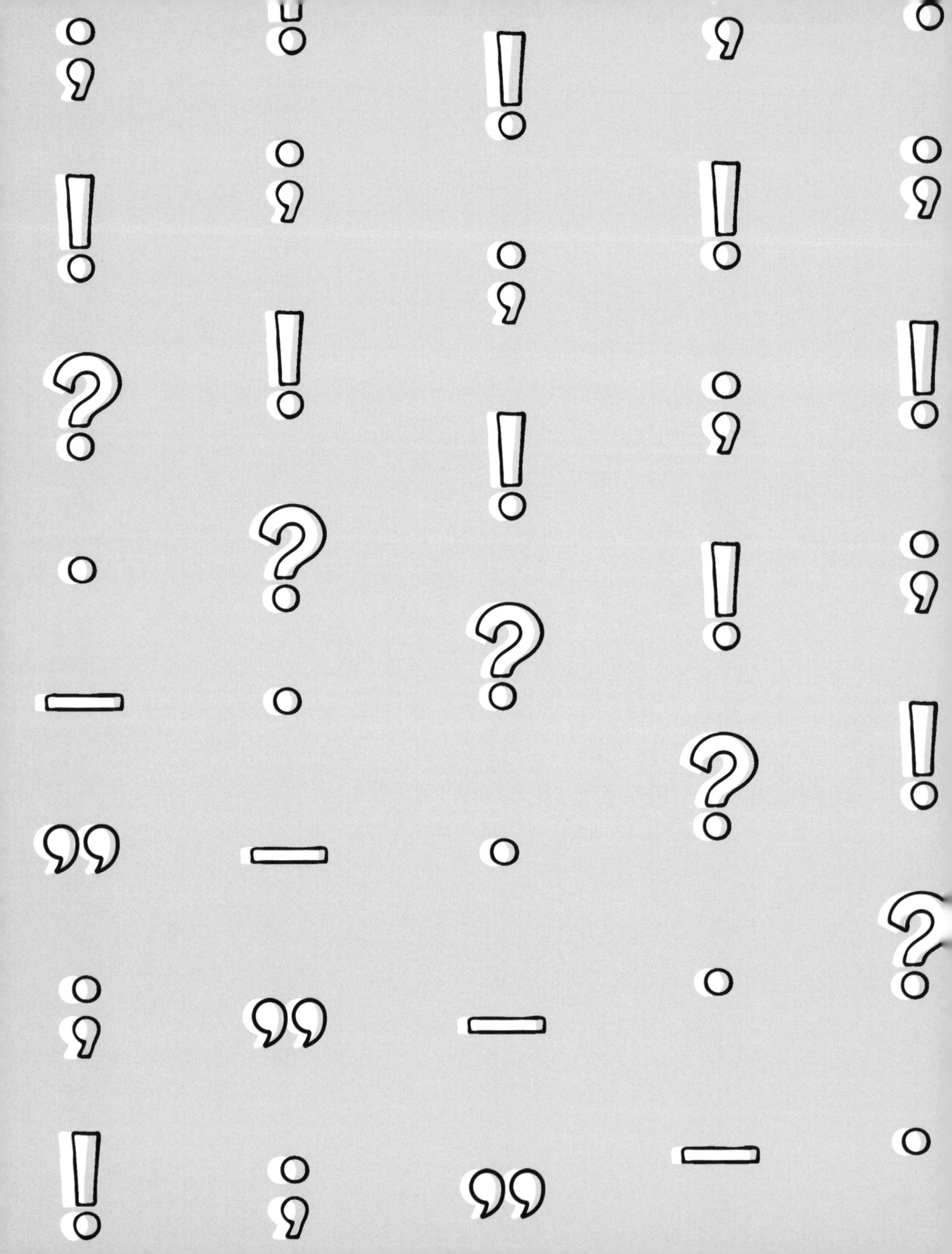

Chapter Eight

Sentences and Punctuation

Now that we've looked at the various types of words and tenses in English, let's put them to practical use in sentences. A **sentence** is a complete thought in English, like *I took an exam.* Those four words form a sentence, which expresses a complete idea. If I said *I took,* you would be wondering, did he take a bus or the last donut? Did he take some time to do something, like a break or a ride? **Punctuation** refers to the various marks (. -, ; ?) that we use to show where a sentence begins, pauses, and ends and that help to make the meaning of our sentences clear.

Basic Sentence Structure and Clauses

A basic sentence in English represents a complete thought, or **independent clause**, and is generally made up of at least a subject and a verb.

1. UFOs fly.
2. The woman is working.
3. The Empire State Building is iconic.

A sentence containing an independent clause can exist by itself because it has a complete meaning.

1. This factory produces cars.
2. The university library has over one million books.
3. Some employees have a four-day workweek.

A **dependent clause** can also contain a subject and a verb, but its meaning is incomplete. Let's look at an example:

This factory produces cars, which are exported to the United States.

In this sentence, "this factory produces cars" is an independent clause, and "which are exported to the United States" is the dependent clause. The dependent clause is literally *depending* on the independent clause to give it meaning, so even though it contains a subject and a verb, the clause "which are exported to the United States" by itself has an incomplete meaning.

Exercise 53
Now it's your turn to practice.

Decide if the clause is an independent or dependent clause.

1. I think I have finally found the answer.
2. In the middle of the park where the pond is.
3. She asked me for a lift.
4. Where you can find the parts factory.
5. That she can submit her résumé.

Compound and Complex Sentences

A **compound sentence** is made up of two independent clauses that are connected.

1. The woman is working, but she is enjoying her work.
2. The Empire State Building is iconic; it was the tallest building in New York City for forty years.
3. Even though UFOs fly, they are not the only things that do so.

A **complex sentence** is made up of one independent clause and one or more dependent clauses. The dependent clause provides extra information about the independent clause. Let's look at an example:

The woman is working in her office, which is located on Rodeo Drive.

In this example, "the woman is working in her office" is the independent clause, and "which is located on Rodeo Drive" is the dependent clause. Here are a few more examples:

1. Domenica's office is on Rodeo Drive, where you can find a number of shops, restaurants, and small offices.
2. Professor Horowitz came to the conference even though he had a cold.
3. The annual report will be published when the CFO gives his final approval.

Exercise 54
Now it's your turn to practice.

In each sentence, underline the independent clause and circle the dependent clause.

1. Even though Manuel had the necessary experience and qualifications, he was turned down for the job.
2. We recorded the CEO's speech, which he gave at the conference.
3. Carson wasn't able to pass the final exam because he didn't put enough effort into studying.
4. Yumi likes to study in the public library, which has a number of private study rooms.
5. We won't be able to start the meeting until everyone has arrived at the office.

Adjective Clauses, Noun Clauses, and Adverbial Clauses

There are three types of dependent clauses: **Adjective clauses** begin with a **relative pronoun** (*that, which, who, whom,* or *whose*) or a **relative adverb** like *when* and *where*. Adjective clauses also contain a verb (or a subject and verb) and give us more information about the noun they follow. *That* is for when you're identifying the subject of the sentence: "The pizza box had a label that named me the owner." *Which* is for nonessential clauses in a sentence: "The pizza, which I ordered online, meant everything to me."

1. I applied to a number of schools, but NYU is the only one **that gave me a scholarship**.
2. I haven't met the people **who work in the accounting department yet**.
3. Jay works in an office **where everyone has to wear a suit**.

Noun clauses begin with a question word (*who, what, when, where, which, why,* or *how*) and conjunctions like *if, whether,* and *that*. Noun clauses act like nouns, and as such, they can be used as the subject or object of the verb.

1. Do you know **when the midterm exams start**?
2. **Why he decided to quit his job** is a mystery to me.
3. It was obvious to everyone **that Tatiana deserved that promotion**.

Adverb clauses begin with a conjunction like *although, because, once, unless, until,* and *while*. We use adverb clauses to indicate where, when, why, or how as well as a condition, contrast, or result.

1. Please don't use your cell phone **while you are working**.
2. **Because Chantara put in a lot of effort**, she was named salesperson of the year.
3. **Once you go through orientation**, you'll be assigned a username and password.

Awkward Mistakes to Avoid
Don't Press Send!

Knowing when to use *who* and *whom* all comes down to one thing: Are you talking about the subject of the sentence or the object?

If it's the subject, use *who*: *Who* likes pizza? Everyone does.

If it's the object, use *whom*: This pizza belongs to *whom*? Me.

Complete the sentence using an adjective, noun, or adverb clause.

1. I remember a time _____ .
2. Can you tell me _____ ?
3. _____ , we won't be able to finish this project.
4. The boss asked me to work this weekend _____ .
5. Technology, _____ , advances at an incredible rate these days.

Commas, Hyphens, Dashes, and Apostrophes

We use **commas** to separate parts of a sentence to make the meaning clear. Notice how the meaning of the sentence can change depending on how a comma is used or not used:

1. Eat, Jimmy. *Here we are trying to encourage Jimmy to eat.*
2. Eat Jimmy. *Here we are suggesting what to eat: Jimmy!*
3. Now, we're going to hit, guys. *Here, we are instructing the guys about the next part of a game.*
4. Now we're going to hit guys. *Here we are explaining what is going to be hit: the guys.*

In compound sentences, we use commas before conjunctions (like *but, so,* and *and*) that connect independent clauses.

1. Being a YouTuber can be fun and exciting, but not everyone can make a living doing it.
2. My friend wanted to go into accounting, so he went back to school to get a master's degree.
3. Masashi is a well-known cardiologist, and his wife is a pediatrician.

We use **hyphens** to form some compound words and to divide words at the end of a line on a page.

As we saw on page 12, we use hyphens to form compound adjectives from numbers, like *five-day workweek*. There are also a number of adjectives and nouns in English that are formed with a hyphen. Here are some examples:

deep-fried	merry-go-round	time-out
dry-cleaning	part-time	x-ray
long-winded	president-elect	

We also use hyphens to describe age and write numbers and fractions. Numbers higher than ninety-nine do not need a hyphen.

one-third	six-eighths	fifty-seven
one-half	twenty-two	eighty-nine

We use hyphens to connect certain prefixes (*anti, pre, pro, post,* etc.) with proper nouns.

anti-Nazi	pre-Christmas
post-Brexit	pro-Palestinian

A hyphen is also used at the end of a line when using a specific margin, like in the following example:

When you are writing on a computer and there is a long sentence, the computer may insert a hyphen, dividing a word by its syllable.

An **em dash**, which is the widest dash, is used in informal English to separate extra information in a sentence for emphasis. It can replace parentheses and commas in many sentences.

1. All of the people in my office—from the manager to the receptionist—work a five-day workweek.
2. We worked for many hours—many long hours—to finish the report on time.

We use **apostrophes** to form possessive nouns and indefinite pronouns, contractions, and some plurals.

Form the possessive form of a noun or indefinite pronoun with an apostrophe followed by *s.*

anyone**'s** idea	the company**'s** policy	the résumé**'s** header
the CEO**'s** speech	the dog**'s** tail	someone**'s** report
Charlie**'s** presentation	everybody**'s** exam result	the tablet**'s** charger

When a plural noun or a proper noun ends in *s,* the possessive is formed by just adding an apostrophe.

Arkansas**'** population	teachers**'** office
the Joneses**'** cat	zoos**'** animals

Correctly modify the sentences in the following paragraph by adding or deleting commas, hyphens, dashes, and apostrophes. Capitalize as necessary.

The First-Day on the Job

Today was the first day of work for the part time and full time trainees at Acme Corporations headquarters in LA. Even though everyones mood was upbeat and they were open minded many of them were a little on edge. One of the trainees tasks was to read the companys HR handbook the whole handbook! Its over thirty five chapters. Actually they were given ample time to complete the task and some of the trainers were on standby to assist them.

Colons and Semicolons

Generally, **colons** follow independent clauses and go before a list, a direct quote, or an **appositive**, which is a phrase that modifies a noun.

We use a colon before a list. When doing so, separate the items in the list with *and* or commas.

1. Make sure you bring the following on the day of your TOEFL exam: your confirmation e-mail from ETS and a valid form of ID.
2. Once you register for the conference, you will receive an attendee kit containing: a name badge, a badge holder, a floor plan of the conference hall, and a tote bag.

When the colon is followed by a sentence, begin with an uppercase letter. When the colon is not followed by a sentence, begin with a lowercase letter.

1. The company policy is very clear: All vacation requests must be submitted at least two weeks in advance.
2. There are only two possible grades you can receive in this class: pass or fail.

We use a colon before a direct quote when we do not use phrases like *she said* or *they said*.

1. I'll never forget what my statistics teacher told me: "Your last mistake is your best teacher."
2. Skyler said that Benjamin Franklin's famous words inspired her to become a teacher: "Tell me and I forget, teach me and I may remember, involve me and I learn."

We use a colon before an appositive, which adds more information to the preceding noun.

1. Ibrahim was in awe when he came face-to-face with the largest land animal in the world: the African elephant.
2. A boss needs to exhibit certain qualities: trust in their employees and the ability to motivate staff.

We use a **semicolon** to connect two independent clauses closely related in meaning.

1. Some bosses take good care of their employees; they help them develop their skills and grow in the company.
2. Many children are interested in learning coding these days; in fact, many schools now offer coding and programming classes.

We also use semicolons to separate a series of items that contain commas.

1. Many students wonder if they should buy a tablet, which is very portable; a laptop, which has a keyboard; or a desktop, which has the most memory and storage of the three.
2. I've worked in three countries in Asia: China, where I taught English; Japan, where I worked as a voice actor; and South Korea, where I was a university professor.

Correctly modify the sentences by adding or deleting the colons or semicolons. Add capitalization, commas, or periods as necessary.

1. Ana graduated from university in three and a half years her next goal is to pass the CPA exam.
2. We need to set up the conference room with the equipment for the meeting the projector the remote control and the screen.
3. There are three ways to grow your business social media which will attract potential customers a mailing list to keep in touch with current customers and a website to provide information about your business.
4. Many new managers face the same problem they try to keep the same relationships that they had before becoming a manager.
5. I'll never forget what my grandfather used to tell me always keep your sense of humor and never worry about anything you can't control.

Parentheses and Brackets

We use **parentheses** to indicate extra information that may be useful for the reader.

1. Anyone applying for an office job needs to know basic office software (Word, Excel, PowerPoint) and have good communication skills.
2. The Edo Period (1603–1868) was a Japanese historical period in which the country was closed to almost all foreign trade.

We also use parentheses with the numbers and letters of a list.

1. During your annual performance review, your manager will discuss (1) your sales results for the year, (2) your goals for the following year, and (3) your career path.
2. For the final exam, you can choose from either (a) a multiple-question exam or (b) a three-page essay.

We use square **brackets** in editing to show something that was added and square brackets with three dots to show that something was deleted.

1. There are many international companies […] which manufacture those components.
2. In fact, Salisbury Construction [the only LEAD-certified construction firm in the area] had taken over operations of the project.

Add parentheses as needed in the following sentences.

1. Her research described the effects of Prohibition 1920–1933 on the New York City economy.
2. To enter the building, you need to 1 show a photo ID, 2 pass through the metal detector, and 3 pass through the facial recognition scanner.

In the following sentences, add or delete information and indicate your edits using brackets.

1. The three major automakers use parts produced by a number of factories in Mexico.
2. The volume of work produced by Natsume Sōseki one of the most famous figures in Japanese literature rivals that of Franz Kafka.

Quotation Marks

Quotation marks in English are always used in pairs, at the top of the line, and with the curve of both marks pointed toward the words being quoted. We generally use quotation marks to indicate direct reported speech. We usually separate the quoted sentence or phrase using a comma. Note that all of the punctuation marks related to the quote are placed inside the quotation marks.

1. She said**,** "I'm impressed with the security in this office**."**
2. "Please take the elevator to the tenth floor**,**" said the receptionist**,** "and then turn left**."**
3. "Stop**!**" she said**.** "I'm tired of your excuses**."**
4. "Where is the meeting room**?**" Kim asked.

Other punctuation marks, which are not part of the quote, go outside the quotation marks.

1. Did she say**,** "I'm not going to go"**?**
2. What does he mean when he says "I'm knackered"**?**

We use a single quotation mark when we enclose a quote inside another quote.

1. The nurse replied, **"**The doctor said, **'**You should stop smoking,**'** but the man refused.**"**
2. Jay's dad said, **"**Jay, have fun at the party and say **'**congratulations**'** to Wilma for me.**"**

Exercise 59
Now it's your turn to practice.

Decide if quotation marks and other related punctuation marks are used correctly. Correct any errors.

"Have a seat, Mr. Jameson", said the lawyer. "This won't take long".

Mr. Jameson sat back on the sofa. He had a curious look on his face, and he could not understand why they were staring at him. He looked right at the lawyer's face and said: "Let's get to the point: What do you want me to do?"

"Its important for us to find the truth. A man's life is at stake," replied the lawyer.

Jameson looked down for a moment and then their eyes met. "I think the truth is clear," "don't you?"

"What exactly," chimed the lawyer ", is clear? We want to hear that from you."

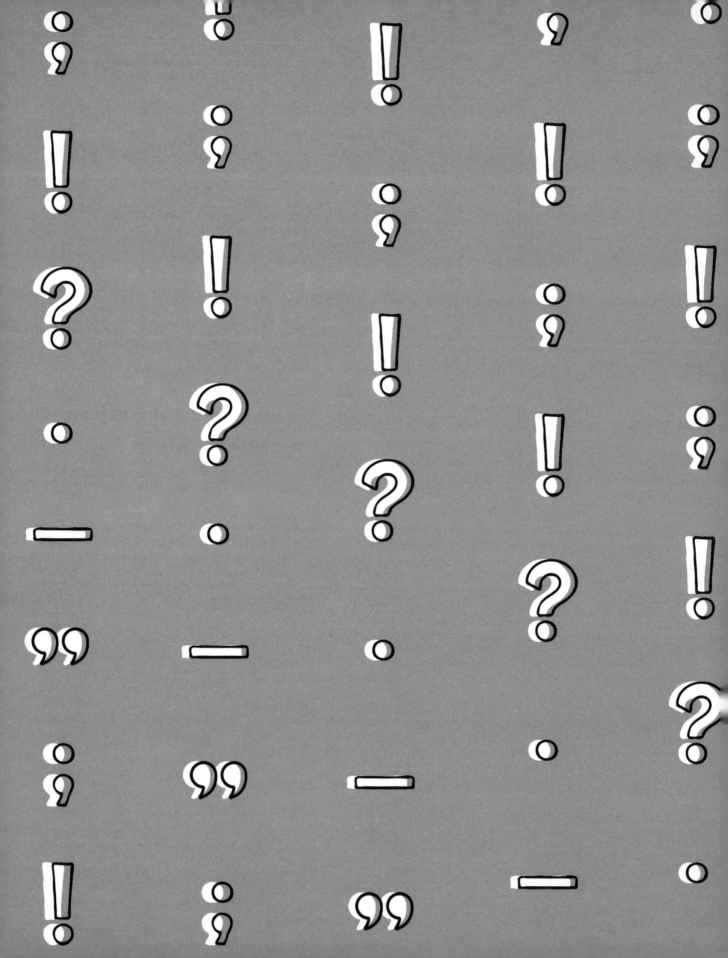

Chapter Nine

Usage and Style

Now that we've looked at the various types of sentences, it's time to see how we use them. First, we'll look at the two basic categories of sentences, how they indicate actions, and the results of those actions. Then we'll explore various ways you can improve your writing to make your sentences clear and logical, including how to adjust the style of your sentences to fit the audience you are writing for and how to avoid missteps in your writing that may obscure the meaning.

Active and Passive Voice

English sentences can be classified into two categories: active and passive. In an active sentence, also called the **active voice**, the emphasis is on who or what is doing the action.

1. The chairman **is leading** the meeting.
2. My teacher **has graded** our exams.
3. The software **analyzes** the data.
4. Many people all over the world **speak** English.

In a passive sentence, also called the **passive voice**, the emphasis is on the result of the action—who or what did the action is either unimportant or unknown. The structure is the *be* verb followed by the past participle (for example: *is made, was created, is being done, had been completed*, etc.).

1. The meeting **is being led** by the chairman.
2. The exams **have been** graded by the teacher.
3. The data **is analyzed** by the software.
4. English **is spoken** all over the world.

When the sentence mentions people, especially people we know, we prefer to use the active voice. It is more natural to say, "My husband cooked dinner" than it is to say, "Dinner was cooked by my husband."

The passive voice can only be formed with **transitive verbs**: those verbs that can take a direct object. **Intransitive verbs**, like *happen, seem, die*, etc., cannot be used in the passive voice. You can say "An accident happened" but not "An accident was happened."

Exercise 60
Now it's your turn to practice.

In the following sentences, change the active sentences to passive and the passive sentences to active if possible.

Active	Passive
1. Eli completed the report.	
2. A problem occurred with the transaction.	
3.	The issue was solved by the student advisor.
4.	These scanners are made in China.
5.	J. S. Bach was born in 1685.

Double Negatives

A double negative occurs when the adverb *not* occurs in a sentence with another negative word such as *nobody, never, hardly,* or *rarely.* Since you can only have one negative word in an English sentence, double negatives are incorrect and, as such, not used.

1. We **never don't** finish our tasks ... *should be written as* ... We never finish our tasks.
2. She **doesn't hardly** study for exams ... *should be written as* ... She hardly studies for exams.
3. Eleanor **isn't rarely** on time for work ... *should be written as* ... Eleanor is rarely on time for work.

However, it is possible to use a negative verb followed by a negative adjective.

1. He **wasn't uncooperative**, but he wasn't forthcoming with information.
2. According to the professor, that student **isn't unhappy** with her grade, but she's not exactly thrilled by it, either.

Exercise 61
Now it's your turn to practice.

In the following sentences, decide whether the use of the negative is correct and if not, make the necessary corrections.

1. It seems like no one was ready to hear that news.
2. Todd said he doesn't never travel by bus because he gets motion sickness.
3. The previous manager wasn't unkind, but he wasn't the friendliest person, either.
4. I don't seldom have the opportunity to have such a productive meeting.
5. I haven't done nothing to bother him, so I have no idea why he's angry.

First and Third Person

When you write, the first thing to decide is the point of view, which refers to the perspective from which the writing is coming. These two perspectives are known as **the first person** and **the third person**.

The first-person point of view uses the pronoun *I* and tells the story from the perspective of the writer or speaker. The first-person point of view is used primarily in personal writing, such as a diary or journal.

It was a really cold day, and I was only wearing a light jacket.

This type of personal writing can also be found in personal essays, when you are asked your opinion about something.

I think the main themes in "The Raven" by Edgar Allan Poe are grief and loss.

This point of view tends to sound very subjective, and because of that, it is not appropriate in academic writing.

With the third-person point of view, the writer or speaker does not refer to himself or herself. The third-person perspective uses the pronouns *he, she,* and *it,* and as such, the writing or speaking sounds more objective.

In his article about the Japanese novel *The Tale of Genji,* Buruma writes that in those days, "a sense of style" was most important to a noble gentleman.

In this example, the writer states their assessment objectively and provides an academic source as evidence. This is the appropriate style for use in academic writing. Using the first-person *I* would only be acceptable when discussing or introducing your own research.

> ## Exercise 62
> ## Now it's your turn to practice.

Write a one-paragraph summary of a book, movie, TV program, or video game using the first-person perspective. Then rewrite the summary using the third-person perspective.

Wordiness

Sometimes, our message can get lost among the words we use. Wordiness, in particular, means that some of the words or phrases you used were unnecessary. Here are examples of how to avoid wordiness:

Try to avoid redundant or meaningless words.

It's not necessary to use the phrase *past history* because all history is in the past. So, instead of saying "Let's look at the *past history* of this issue," just say "Let's look at the *history* of this issue." Here are a few more examples:

combine together…*should be*…combine
current status…*should be*…status
final outcome…*should be*…outcome
on a daily basis…*should be*…daily
summarize briefly…*should be*…summarize
twelve noon…*should be*…noon

Look for more precise vocabulary.

1. Instead of saying *in spite of the fact that,* say *although.*
2. Instead of saying *put off the meeting,* say *postpone the meeting.*
3. Instead of saying *we are of the opinion that,* say *we believe.*

Avoid qualifiers like *barely, extremely, hardly, quite,* and *very.*

1. Instead of saying *barely legible,* say *illegible.*
2. Instead of saying *hardly noticeable,* say *faint.*
3. Instead of saying *quite shy,* say *timid.*

Exercise 63
Now it's your turn to practice.

Rewrite the following memo, making it less wordy and more concise.

Notice to All of Our Employees

In spite of the fact that we have a number of official rules regarding the company's written attendance policy, quite a few employees working here tend to usually arrive at the office late. Because of that fact, the company president, who by the way is very upset about this, has asked me to touch base with every single one of our employees and inform them of this point. In the event that you are late for work more than three different occurrences, you will face the possibility of termination of your employment.

Misplaced Words and Sentence Logic

The way you arrange the words in a sentence can have a significant effect on the clarity and meaning of your writing. Here are categories of misplaced words and phrases that you should try to avoid:

Dangling modifiers are phrases that cause ambiguity because they refer to the wrong word in a sentence.

1. Walking in the park, a tree fell in front of me. ← *Was the tree walking in the park?*
2. Looking out the office window, the Empire State Building was magnificent. ← *Was the Empire State Building looking out the office window?*
3. Wanting some fresh air, the hiking trip was quickly organized. ← *Was the hiking trip wanting some fresh air?*

Misplaced modifiers are words that are ambiguously placed and make the meaning unclear.

1. The boss only reprimands the sales staff. ← *Nobody else reprimands the sales staff? The boss doesn't reprimand other teams in the office?*
2. He told me the story of his business trip last week. ← *Did he tell me the story last week, or was his business trip last week?*
3. Just tell me what to do. ← *Am I asking you to only tell me what to do and not tell me anything else, or am I asking you to tell me and not anyone else?*

Misplaced phrases are phrases that are ambiguously placed and make the meaning unclear.

1. Everyone in the office was excited to learn that they had reached the monthly sales goal from the CEO's letter. ← *What came from the CEO's letter, the news about reaching the monthly sales goal or the sales goal itself?*
2. I read that it's going to snow tomorrow on the Internet. ← *Is it going to snow on the Internet, or is the Internet where I got the information?*
3. The employee was fired when it was discovered the money was stolen by the shop manager. ← *Was it the employee or the shop manager who stole the money?*

Split infinitives occur when an adverb is incorrectly placed between *to* and the verb, causing confusion.

1. I arranged to quickly go there and help them.
2. I began to suddenly feel tired.
3. I decided finally to look for a new job.

Exercise 64
Now it's your turn to practice.

Correct all of the ambiguity in the following sentences.

1. Walking away from the counter, the coffee cup fell on the floor.
2. His talking quickly made me confused.
3. Washing your hands often helps prevent colds.
4. I think my sister only knows my mom's recipes.
5. I read that the CEO is going to give a speech in the company newsletter.

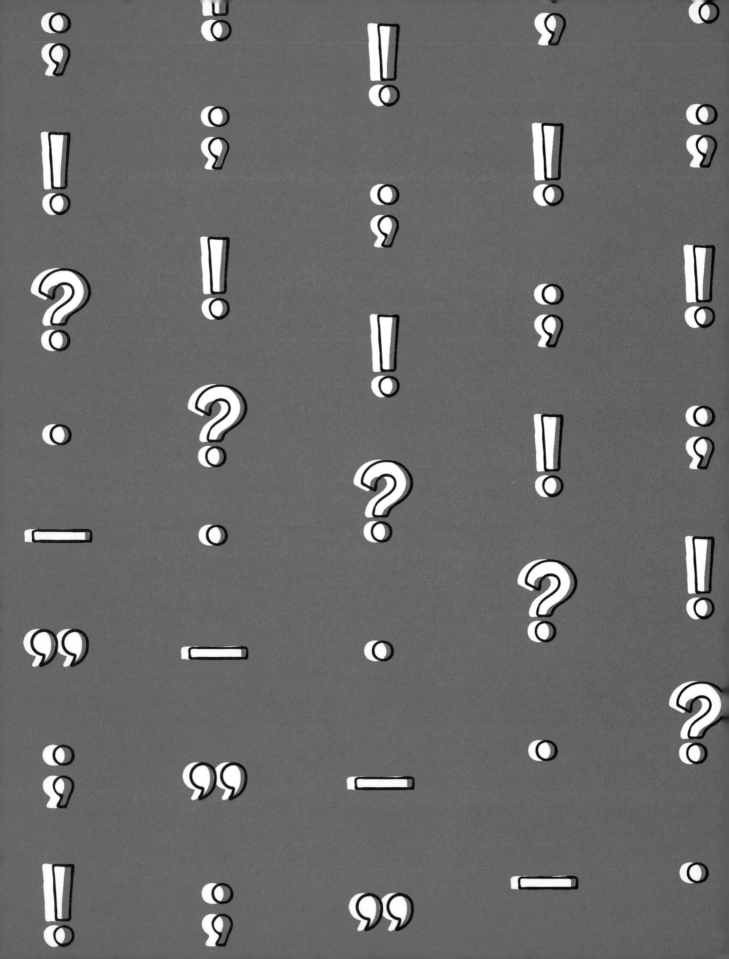

Chapter Ten

The Paragraph

Paragraphs are the building blocks of written English. Each paragraph in an essay or academic report expresses a complete idea, which is usually based on a theme expressed in the opening sentence of the paragraph. A paragraph should be focused on one idea, and a good paragraph in English has three parts: a topic sentence, several supporting sentences, and a concluding sentence.

Topic Sentence

The **topic sentence** indicates to the reader what the paragraph is about and forms the basis on which you will write the rest of your paragraph. A good topic sentence should be clear, concise, informative, and interesting. Here are some examples of topic sentences:

1. A city has many attractions to keep its residents entertained.
2. The best way for the university to spend its surplus budget is to upgrade the library.
3. Learning from a teacher is more efficient than learning by experience.

You may be writing a paragraph or an essay in response to a question prompt. Here are some examples of TOEFL-style prompts and their corresponding topic sentences:

1. Prompt: If you could change one important thing about your hometown, what would you change?

Topic sentence: I would like to increase the number of parks and recreational facilities in my hometown.

2. Prompt: Do you agree or disagree with the following statement? *Television has destroyed communication among friends and family.*

Topic sentence: I agree that television has destroyed communication among friends and family.

3. Prompt: Some people prefer to live in a small town. Others prefer to live in a big city. Which would you prefer?

Topic sentence: I prefer to live in a big city.

Based on the given topics, write a paragraph topic sentence.

1. Prompt: Why do you think people like extreme sports, like hang gliding or ice climbing?

Topic sentence:

2. Prompt: Would you support or oppose a plan to build a new shopping mall in your town?

Topic sentence:

3. Prompt: Do you prefer working from home or working from your office?

Topic sentence:

Paragraph Body

After you write your topic sentence, you're going to support your thesis in the **body** of the paragraph. The sentences following the topic sentence must support the topic sentence in a logical way. Let's look at an example of some support for a topic sentence.

A city has many attractions to keep its residents entertained. Cities have cultural institutions, such as art galleries and museums, where you can experience art, history, science, and more. In addition, most cities have theaters and concert halls where you can see a play, musical, or concert. Nightlife options in a city, such as bars and clubs, provide places for people to socialize, and restaurants give people a variety of dining options. All of these provide plenty of leisure-time activities for city dwellers.

Let's analyze the paragraph.

The topic sentence declares, "A city has many attractions to keep its residents entertained." Following this are three concise support sentences:

1. Cities have cultural institutions, such as art galleries and museums, where you can experience art, history, science, and more.
2. In addition, most cities have theaters and concert halls where you can see a play, musical, or concert.

3. Nightlife options in a city, such as bars and clubs, provide places for people to socialize, and restaurants give people a variety of dining options.

Each of these support sentences provides an example of something related to that first topic sentence: "A city has many attractions to keep its residents entertained."

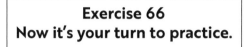

Exercise 66
Now it's your turn to practice.

Write a paragraph including a topic sentence and supporting sentences based on one of the following prompts.

1. What was the greatest invention of the twentieth century?
2. Where is your favorite place to study?
3. What is the most important issue facing society today?
4. What is the best way to get around in your city or town?

Paragraph Conclusion

Once you have written your topic sentence and the sentences supporting your thesis, you'll conclude the paragraph with a sentence that summarizes the contents. Let's look at the paragraph and concluding sentence from the last lesson:

1. The topic sentence stated the thesis: "A city has many attractions . . ."
2. The supporting sentences provided some examples: cultural institutions, theaters and concert halls, and nightlife.
3. The conclusion summarized the whole paragraph: "All of these provide plenty of leisure-time activities for city dwellers."

Exercise 67
Now it's your turn to practice.

Using the paragraph you wrote for Exercise 66, write a concluding sentence.

Transition Words

Transition words connect the sentences and ideas in a paragraph in a smooth and logical way. Transition words are categorized based on their function.

Contrast words show dissimilarity between ideas.

although	however	on the other hand
but	nevertheless	while

1. Having a new shopping center would be good for the local economy. **However**, it would cause an increase in traffic congestion.
2. **While** technology has given us more options for communication, it has also provided criminals with new ways to scam their victims.

Example words help organize paragraphs by introducing and illustrating examples or reasons.

as well as	first, second, etc.	furthermore
finally	for instance	such as

1. Cities have many attractions to keep their residents entertained. **For instance**, cultural institutions **such as** art galleries and museums give us the opportunity to experience art, history, and science.
2. Nightlife options in a city, **such as** bars and clubs, provide places for people to socialize, and restaurants give people a variety of dining options.

There are also transition words that show **emphasis**.

certainly	in fact	moreover
indeed	more importantly	surely

1. Social media opens the door to meeting a wide group of people. **In fact**, some social media platforms allow us to connect with celebrities and other famous people.
2. Indeed, a new shopping center would cause an increase in traffic congestion. **Moreover**, this would lead to increased air pollution.

Other transition words can lead us to logical **conclusions**.

as a result	in summary
consequently	thus

1. **In summary**, technology gives people many more ways to communicate than before.
2. **As a result**, people can communicate more often, in more places, and to more people than ever before.

Exercise 68
Now it's your turn to practice.

Enhance the following paragraph using transition words, and add your own concluding sentence.

Technology has given us more options for communication. Mobile phones allow people to communicate with others regardless of their physical location. Text messaging provides a way to instantly contact a friend or family member. Social media gives us the opportunity to reach a wide group of people at one time. Platforms such as YouTube make it easy for anyone to broadcast their ideas and opinions to a global audience.

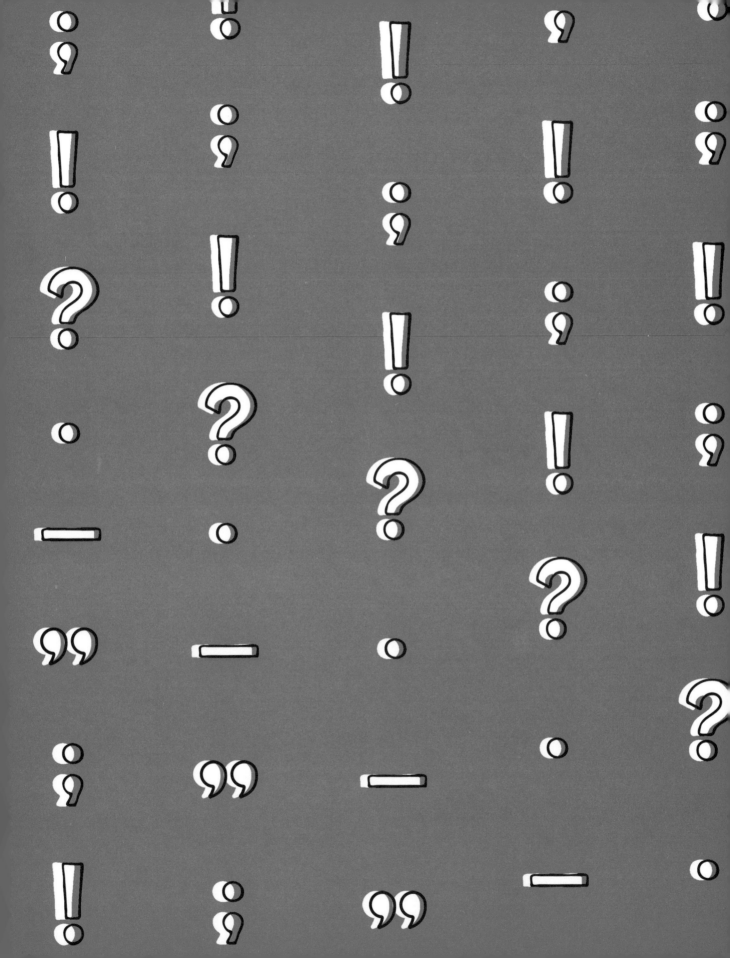

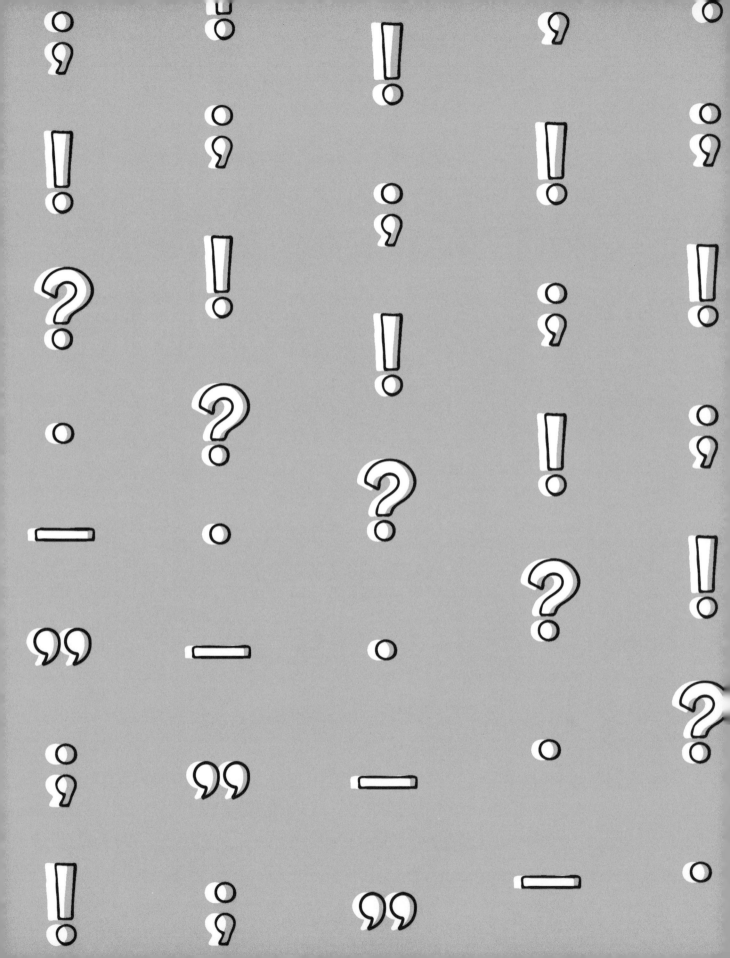

PART TWO

WRITING IN YOUR EVERYDAY LIFE

Congratulations! You've made it to part two, which means you've survived my grammar lessons. Now we'll explore how you can use what you learned in part one in the real world. Different types of writing require different style types. For example, in a message to a friend, you can be informal—you can use abbreviations, contractions, and emojis. However, in a critical paper, you'd need to be more formal and academic, which means no contractions and perhaps even a more elevated vocabulary. In this part, I have selected topics from the business world, academia, and common social situations so you'll get the opportunity to practice different types of English writing, from casual text messages to formal business letters and academic papers. The final section looks at how changes in technology are continuously reshaping how we communicate and the type of language we can use in the modern world.

Remember that no matter how amazing your thoughts are, if you present them in a confusing or incoherent way, readers won't understand. Knowing the rules of grammar and how to apply them will help you put your best foot forward in terms of people understanding exactly what you mean to say.

Chapter Eleven

School

Writing an essay requires planning and organization, and the language we use in an essay for school needs to be more formal than the language we would typically use in conversations or digital communication. In this chapter, we'll explore college admission essays, TOEFL exam essays, and research papers. If you are planning on taking the TOEFL exam, you'll need to write an essay that demonstrates your ability to express your opinion clearly and use a variety of vocabulary and grammar. Research papers are the most formal of the three types of writing we'll cover in this section.

College Admissions Essays

The essay you write for college admissions will give the school its first impression of you and your communication skills. The two most popular types of college admissions essay prompts are (1) Tell us about yourself and (2) Why do you want to go to our school?

When the essay topic is of the "Tell us about yourself" variety, the school is not interested in how your mom would answer the question, such as "she likes strawberry ice cream" or "he's very good at sports." Instead, it's a good idea to write about your passions, interests, experiences, after-school activities, etc., as they relate to your intended area of study. This kind of essay is designed for you to tell a story about who you are and how you got here. Here's an example of the opening of an essay from a student interested in coding and programming:

> *Grand Theft Auto* was the first game I ever played. Of course, playing the game itself was exciting, but for me, there was something intriguing far beyond Franklin's street smarts. The fact that I was able to navigate in this virtual world with just a controller captured my attention. I became fascinated with the idea of the inner workings behind the scenes, especially the programming languages.

The writer could then continue by describing her related experiences, such as taking programming classes online, participating in a coding club after school, etc.

The next type of question, "Why do you want to go to our school?," is an invitation for you to explain what about this particular school has piqued your interest enough for you to want to study there. It's not enough to say something like "I chose the University of Miami because I want to live in a warm place" or "Your school has a great basketball team." It's essential to first research the school carefully to make sure they offer a course of study that matches your goals. What is it about this school that stimulates your interest? If the college has a major and courses that align with your career goals, you'll want to write an essay that illustrates that. Here's an example:

> I've always been interested in broadcasting, so I am seeking a career in radio. When I came across the description of your Voice and Diction course, it opened my eyes to the fact that we can learn to control our accent and pronunciation to better engage with listeners on the air.

> **Now it's your turn to practice.**

Using what you learned about paragraphs, develop a paragraph (including the topic sentence, supporting sentences, and conclusion) for one of the essay prompts in this section.

TOEFL Independent Essays

The TOEFL exam, used by most American colleges and universities to gauge an international student's English ability, includes several writing tasks. However, the independent essay is the only task that gives you complete control over your answer and your grade for this part of the exam. By practicing to write a good TOEFL essay, you can help increase your score and simultaneously prepare yourself for the writing assignments you'll get once in school.

The independent essay is based on a question about your opinion on a topic. Some examples are:

1. Which would you prefer, living in a big city or living in the countryside?
2. Would you support or oppose a movie theater being built in your neighborhood?
3. Has technology destroyed communication between friends or family members?

You'll have thirty minutes to complete the task, giving you about five minutes to outline your essay, twenty minutes to write it, and then five minutes to review the essay for errors. Your essay will be scored on idea development, organization, and use of language.

A good essay for this section of the exam will have three basic parts:

1. An introductory paragraph, where you state your opinion.
2. A body, with two or three paragraphs supporting your opinion.
3. A conclusion summarizing the key points of your essay.

Let's look at these three parts using this prompt: Which would you prefer, living in a big city or living in the countryside?

In the **introductory paragraph**, you need to do two things.

1. First, restate the question in your own words. Try to write at least two sentences about each of the options you are given. Here is an example:

Some people feel that living in a big city is exciting. Big cities have all of the conveniences of life in one small area. Others may think that life in the countryside is ideal because the air is clean and it is generally quiet.

In the preceding sentences, I restated the question by presenting opinions on both options.

2. Second, write your thesis statement. Your thesis statement is your opinion, including your reasons for that opinion. It will become the basis for the rest of your essay. Here is an example:

I believe that living in the countryside is preferable to living in a big city. While city life might be more convenient and provides opportunities for enjoyment and recreation, cities can be uncomfortable because of poor air quality, noise, and congestion.

In the preceding sentences, I stated my opinion and provided some specific reasons for and against living in a city.

Next, let's take a look at a sample **body paragraph**. Each body paragraph should begin with a statement of one of your reasons and contain at least two sentences supporting that reason. Here is an example:

The air quality in the countryside is much cleaner than that of a big city. With fewer cars and buses in the countryside, exhaust fumes are not an issue. With no factories in the countryside, there is less industrial pollution. Additionally, the abundance of trees and plants in the countryside makes the air fresher and the atmosphere idyllic.

In the preceding paragraph, I stated one of my reasons for preferring life in the countryside: clean air. I then gave several examples to support this idea. The next two body paragraphs should be written in a similar way. For example:

Since the city is densely populated with people and attractions, it tends to be noisier than the countryside. Sounds of car horns and sirens persist day and night. Building construction and roadwork, as well as commercial traffic in the city, add to the noise. The countryside has few or none of these sources of noise, resulting in a more peaceful atmosphere.

Finally, big cities attract a lot of people. In addition to the many people living and working in the city, there are usually many tourists. For example, in New York City, neighborhoods such as Times Square are generally crowded with tourists. With fewer residents and workers and hardly any tourists, the countryside is much less congested than a big city.

Now, let's move on to the **conclusion**. This final paragraph of your essay should:

1. Restate the topic and your opinion.
2. Summarize the points you made in the body paragraphs.

Here is an example:

While it is true that big cities feature many benefits, in my estimation, the disadvantages significantly outweigh the advantages. Life in the countryside is quieter and more secluded than life in a big city. Furthermore, the clean air and idyllic landscape associated with the country can provide a more enjoyable, healthier way of life. In conclusion, life in the countryside is more desirable than life in a big city.

Now it's your turn to practice.

Using what you learned about paragraph structure, write a TOEFL essay based on one of the prompts given in this lesson.

Research Papers

Research papers are an interesting combination of research and independent thinking. Here are the five steps to creating a polished and professional research paper:

1. **Determine your topic.** In most cases, your professor will give you a topic to write about. In other cases, you'll need to choose the topic. If your topic is too broad, narrow down the topic so you can easily find specific research about it.

2. **Conduct research and collect information.** You may find some good information online, but library books, journals, and periodicals can provide you with a wealth of information not readily available online. Print or scan copies of useful pages that you find and keep your research records organized. There is nothing worse than having a few photocopies from a book but not remembering which book those pages came from—you'll need to know so you can cite your references and revisit the source if you need additional information.

3. **Choose your information.** Once you have a sufficient amount of material on hand, read through it and take notes or highlight the sections you may want to use as a basis for your paper. Keep in mind that you'll have to assemble the research that you gather and, using your independent thinking, write the story of that research. The story should have a good balance between your original words and some quotations or key facts directly from the research.

4. **Create an outline.** Your outline will help you organize the paper. In fact, some professors require their students to submit an outline as part of the process. Think about the different sections you will include. For example, if the topic is the Sixteenth Amendment, you may want to organize your paper something like this:

   1. The events leading up to the Sixteenth Amendment
      a) The first personal income tax in 1861
      b) The farmers' revolt and the presidential election of 1892
   2. Prosperity at the turn of the century
      a) The election of Theodore Roosevelt
      b) The graduated income tax
   3. William Howard Taft and the new income tax
   4. How the tax law became an amendment

5. **Write a first draft.** Based on the outline and using your research notes, write the first draft of the research paper. You should start with a thesis statement and an introductory paragraph. For example:

   The road to the Sixteenth Amendment was not paved with silk.

All of the subsequent paragraphs should also be well constructed and contain a topic sentence and supporting evidence. That evidence will include quotations and information from your research.

The research paper should end with a concluding paragraph, where you'll summarize the main points and present your concluding thoughts. The last page should contain a list of the works cited in the paper, formatted according to whichever style (Chicago, MLA, APA, etc.) your professor or school has mandated.

Now it's your turn to practice.

Write an outline for a research paper on any topic that interests you.

Awkward Mistakes to Avoid
Don't Press Send!

Once you've completed your research paper, don't hit Send just yet! Make sure you have done the following before you submit your research project:

Get feedback from your professor on your early drafts.

Make sure the language is appropriate for what you're writing, including spelling, formatting, vocabulary, tone, and citations.

Get a peer review from a classmate or friend.

Make sure you haven't plagiarized.

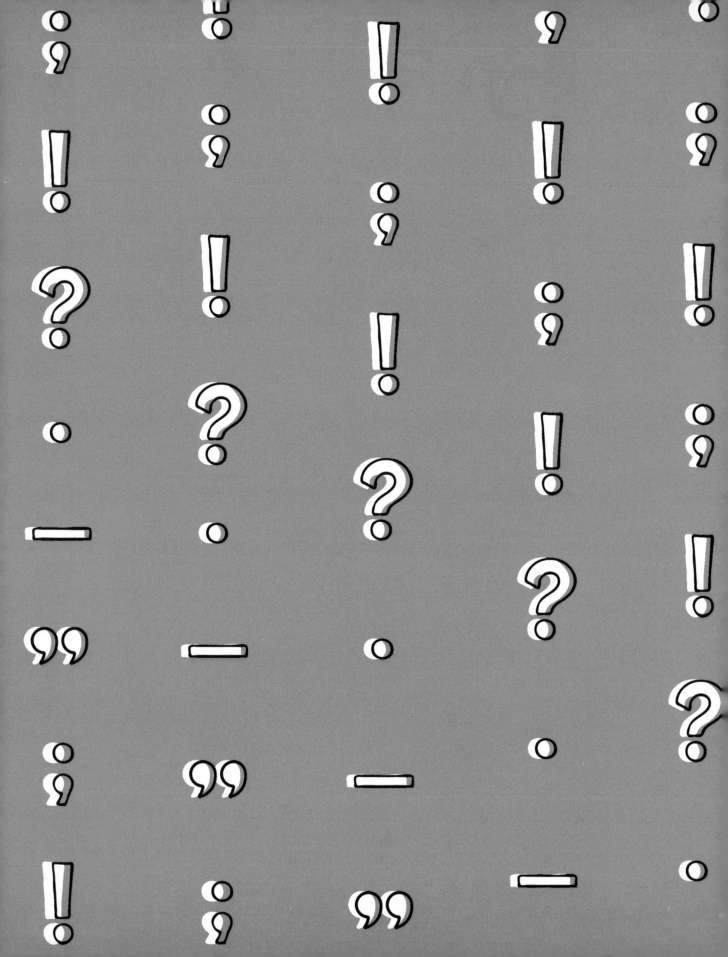

Chapter Twelve

Work

The way we communicate in the workplace is a direct reflection on us. Before you even start the job, your résumé and cover letter will serve as your first impression. Once you land the job, you'll find yourself communicating with others frequently, especially through e-mail or instant messaging. You may also need to make a presentation, evaluate an employee, or negotiate for a desired outcome such as a salary increase. We'll look at these and other common work-related writing tasks, including meeting minutes, website copy, and a tactful letter of resignation.

Perfecting Your Résumé

There are three types of résumés: (1) the chronological résumé, (2) the functional résumé, and (3) the combination résumé.

The **chronological résumé** is most appropriate when you have a long work history. You'll list your work experience in reverse chronological order, with your most recent experience first. After your work history comes your education experience followed by your skills, professional associations, and interests.

A **functional résumé** lists your education, experience, and skills. This résumé is ideal for recent graduates who don't have a lot of work experience or those who have gaps in their work history.

A **combination résumé** is a hybrid of the other two. Here you'll highlight your skills and qualifications first followed by your accomplishments and then your work experience in reverse chronological order.

No matter which type of résumé you go with, follow these guidelines.

- **Write a résumé template.** This is your basic, generic résumé, containing the basics, such as your education and work experience. You will use this template to create a tailored résumé for each job you apply for.
- **Never use the same résumé for every job.** No two positions are exactly the same, and the résumé you send should be customized for that specific job.
- **Make your résumé fit the job.** Look in the job posting and the company website to match your résumé to the position. For example, if you have project management experience, but the advertisement says the company is looking for a project leader, it's fine to change the term "project manager" in your résumé to "project leader." If the job posting lists skills that match your skills, make sure you include them.
- **Include volunteer and life experiences.** Look for relevant connections to your experience. If you're applying to a position that relates to academia and you volunteered in your college library, include that information. If you received an award in your internship, include that, too.

> ## Now it's your turn to practice.

Write your résumé based on the recommendations covered here.

Writing a Cover Letter

We use a cover letter when applying for a job to introduce ourselves and our résumé. The cover letter allows the hiring manager to know what position you are applying for and see a summary of your skills and qualifications.

A cover letter should have about three paragraphs. In the introductory paragraph, respond directly to the advertisement and the job you're applying for in a professional, formal way. Make your purpose clear to the hiring manager. The first paragraph should be customized for each job you apply to.

> I am writing with great enthusiasm in response to the posting on your website for School Director. I possess the following skills and experience that I believe are a perfect match for this position.

The second paragraph should contain a summary of your relevant skills and experience. An effective second paragraph will use key words taken directly from the job posting. Be careful not to make run-on sentences by trying to include all of your relevant information. This initial communication is the first impression you make, so be sure to have succinct, clear sentences with a professional tone.

> I have an MBA in global management and over twenty years of experience in international education, as both a teacher and administrator. Ten of those years have been in various management positions, including work as a school director responsible for a $1 million budget. I am familiar with higher education in the United States, and I enjoy working with students tremendously. I have had extensive experience teaching adult students from all over the world, both in and out of the classroom.

The third paragraph should conclude with essential information for the hiring manager. Be sure to mention the name of the company here.

> Attached is my résumé for your review. It contains the details of the many skills and experiences I can bring to the table for Acme Education. I have also enclosed a list of three professional references. I live in New York, but I am able and willing to relocate. I would welcome the opportunity to interview for this position. Please feel free to reach out via phone or e-mail. In the meantime, thank you for your time and consideration.

Write four or five sentences that describe your skills and experience using the present perfect tense and a professional tone. Here are some examples:

- Ten of my years at ABC *have been* in various management positions.
- I *have had* extensive experience working with students from all over the world.
- I *have enclosed* a list of three professional references.

Writing a Professional E-mail

Since the dawn of text messages, English, like many other languages, has become more casual. The communication style of a comment on Instagram or a text between friends is not appropriate for the business world. It is always better for your e-mails to be more formal than they need to be. The following format is acceptable for a professional business e-mail.

Subject Line

Even though the subject line has been removed from most messaging apps, it is still necessary in a business e-mail. The subject line should concisely describe the topic of your e-mail. Here are some examples:

For a job application to the hiring manager:

Graphic Designer position—Jared Wilson [the job title and your name]

Following up after a job interview:

Thank you for meeting with me.

For a term paper to your professor:

US Tax Laws and the Sixteenth Amendment

To your boss:

Weekly Sales Report

Greetings and Closings

Every e-mail should contain a greeting and closing phrase. Here are the most common forms, listed from formal to informal. Note the comma usage.

Greetings

- Dear Mr. Edison,
- Dear Mr. Thomas Edison,
- Dear Thomas,
- Hi, Thomas,

Closings

- Kind regards,
- Regards,
- Sincerely,
- Thanks,

The body of the e-mail should also be concise. Here are some examples:

E-mail 1

Dear Mr. Edison,
Thank you for taking the time to meet with me this morning. I appreciated the opportunity to learn more about the Graphic Designer position. I look forward to hearing from you about moving ahead in the application process.
Sincerely yours,
Jared Wilson

E-mail 2

Dear Carson,
Please find attached this week's sales report. Let me know if you have any comments or concerns.
Regards,
Danielle

Imagine you are in the following situations and write an e-mail, including the subject line, greeting, closing, and e-mail body.

1. You are sending your résumé to ABC Company to apply for a sales position.
2. You are submitting your research paper to your professor.
3. You are writing to a potential client to set up a meeting.
4. You are writing to a coworker to ask about the schedule for a meeting.

Preparing a Presentation

You may be asked to give a presentation in an academic or professional setting, but the basic idea for both is the same. A presentation is essentiality a one-point lesson in which you convey an idea to your audience. The first step in preparing a presentation is to know who the audience will be. Are you presenting your graduate thesis to a faculty panel? Are you making a sales presentation to potential customers? Knowing who the audience is will help you understand what they are expecting from your presentation.

The presentation itself should contain three sections: (1) an introduction and welcome, (2) the main points of your talk, and (3) a conclusion.

At the start of the introduction section, greet the audience, introduce yourself, and tell everyone what you're going to discuss during the presentation.

Good morning, everyone. I'm Wang Min, and today I would like to introduce you to my company and show you how our graphic design services can help your business grow.

Organize the main points of your talk in a logical way. If you're doing a presentation to introduce your company, the flow of your talk could be something like this:

A brief company history → your company's position in its industry → the services or products you offer → how your company's services or products match with your audience, etc.

To conclude, summarize the main points, and then, if time permits, you can elicit questions or comments from the audience.

Slideshow Basics

It's always a good idea to have a slide presentation to accompany your talk. Tips for an effective slideshow include the following:

- Each slide should represent a key point in your talk and contain the essential information you are presenting.
- Slides should be written simply and clearly. Try to stick to bullet points and avoid full sentences or paragraphs.
- Make sure illustrations such as charts or graphs are clear and legible.
- Ensure that the font size you use is big enough so it can be seen from the very back of the room.

Whether you choose to use a slideshow or not, practice your presentation using notes or cue cards. During your presentation, you'll want to want to speak expressively and occasionally make eye contact with the audience.

> **Now it's your turn to practice.**

Prepare a short presentation on one of the following topics.

1. Introduce your company to a group of college students who may be interested in applying for a job there.
2. Introduce your college to a group of high school students who may want to apply there.

Providing Praise

In business, one of the most important things anyone can do for employee motivation is recognize a job well done. As a colleague, you can boost someone else by offering thanks or praise for their assistance or good ideas. And if you're a manager, a little positive feedback can go a long way in energizing your staff—you don't need to wait until your company has its annual review period to let your staff know they are important and appreciated.

When someone has done something exceptional in the workplace, let them know right away, either during a meeting with them or via a note or message. For example:

Paola, thanks so much for your effort on the ABC account. The purchasing manager placed an order and said that you were very helpful in helping him make his decision. You're the best! Thanks.

You may have someone on your staff who puts in a lot of effort on a daily basis. In this situation, you can thank them in person or with a simple note.

Nasser, I wanted to let you know that I really appreciate the enthusiasm you have when you work. Your positive attitude and attention to detail are a big help here. Keep up the good work.

Even if you are not a manager, a thank-you to a coworker or a boss who helped you out is always appreciated.

Kai, thanks for backing me up with that difficult customer the other day. I really appreciate it.

| **Now it's your turn to practice.** |

Write a short note to thank the following individuals.

1. A new employee who has made their first sale
2. An employee who completed a project sooner than the deadline
3. A coworker who showed you some Excel shortcuts

Asking for a Raise

It's perfectly acceptable to ask for a raise, especially if it's been a while since you started working or received your last raise. A key point is knowing *when* and *how* to approach your manager for a raise. Informal communication, like a casual-toned instant message to your manager, would be inappropriate. If your company has an annual performance review, however, that might be an ideal time to discuss salary.

The next step is knowing what your position is worth. Do a little research on what people in similar jobs in your industry are earning. If you find you're being underpaid, that substantive information can be useful in negotiating a new salary. On the other hand, if you find that you're already at the top pay level, you may want to discuss a step up in responsibilities commensurate with a pay raise.

You can approach the topic with your boss using professional, evidence-backed language like this:

Approach 1

I'm delighted to be working in the sales department here at ABC Company. Over the past year, I've learned a great deal and have gained valuable skills in sales and presentations. I also believe that my work has contributed to the growth of the company, and I'm particularly proud that I contributed to thirty-three percent of the company's revenue last quarter.

I would appreciate having the opportunity to discuss my salary so that my pay is in line with my work performance.

Approach 2

Over the past year and a half, I have gladly taken on several new roles, including project leader and new hire trainer. I've handled these responsibilities and their challenges in a professional and enthusiastic manner. All the projects I've been assigned have been successfully completed. As such, I would appreciate the chance to discuss a new salary commensurate with my current responsibilities and performance.

> **Now it's your turn to practice.**

Think about your current job. What are your recent successes or new responsibilities, and how would you approach your boss to tie these achievements into a salary discussion?

Providing a Resignation Letter

It's never easy ending a relationship, but sometimes that happens in the business world. If you need to move on from your current position, here are some tips and suggestions to resign gracefully and professionally.

First, you don't want to burn any bridges on the way out. Even if the circumstances causing you to leave are emotionally unpleasant, make a clean break without hurting anyone's feelings. You never know if you will run into your boss or other coworkers in the future, particularly if you are working in a small industry. The boss or team you leave behind will also be able to serve as a reference for you if you need one later.

When writing your resignation letter, address the letter to your boss and let them know your intention at the very beginning.

Dear Frank,
I hereby tender my resignation from the position of graphic designer at ABC Company. My last day of work will be June 3, 2020.

Next, regardless of how you feel about the job, thank your employer for the opportunity you've had. This will help to keep the atmosphere positive.

I want you to know that I appreciate all of the opportunities I've had here at ABC. I've learned a great deal from you about graphic design in the marketing industry.

Finally, let your boss know that you would be happy to leave detailed transition notes to assist whoever will be taking your place.

I would be happy to provide comprehensive notes and/or whatever support you think would be helpful during the transition.
Sincerely yours,
Alfred E. Oldman

Now it's your turn to practice.

Think about somebody you respect. Imagine that person is resigning from their job and write their resignation letter.

Writing Meeting Minutes

After a business meeting, a written record of the meeting is often essential. This record, called the **meeting minutes**, contains a detailed summary of every aspect of the meeting.

The level of formality and contents of the meeting minutes vary by company as well as meeting type. Minutes from board and other executive meetings are the most formal, whereas team meeting minutes tend to be more casual. Regardless of the level of formality, all meeting minutes should include the date and time of the meeting, the members, and the content. Here's a sample outline of meeting minutes:

Acme Widget Co. ← *(company name)*

June 3, 2020 ← *(date of the meeting)*

Opening ← *(Formally state the starting time and the attendees.)*

The annual board meeting was held at ten o'clock in the morning on June 3, 2020.

Present at the meeting were Ms. Bergman, Mr. Lennon, Mr. McCartney, Ms. Joplin, and Ms. Swift.

Approval of prior minutes and agenda ← *(This section is generally for formal meetings.)*

The members unanimously approved the minutes of the meeting on May 3, 2020, as well as the agenda for today's meeting.

Open items ← *(any issues or follow-up from the previous meeting minutes to be discussed)*

1. Mr. Lennon discussed ← *(Summarize the discussion here.)*

New items ← *(new issues from the meeting agenda discussed)*

1. Ms. Bergman suggested ← *(Summarize the discussion here.)*
2. *(Write the summary of the discussion here.)*

Additional items ← *(new issues raised and not from the meeting agenda discussed)*

1. Ms. Joplin proposed ← *(Summarize the discussion here.)*
2. *(Write the summary of the discussion here.)*

Next meeting agenda ← *(the topics for the next meeting)*

1. *(Summarize the discussion here.)*
2. *(Summarize the discussion here.)*

Adjournment / Closing ← *(State the ending time and the date for the next meeting.)*

This meeting was adjourned at eleven o'clock in the morning on June 3, 2020. The next board meeting will take place on July 3, 2020, in this office.
Meeting minutes submitted by: Your Name
Meeting minutes approved by: Their Name

Using the outline on page 135, write the meeting minutes for the meeting you last attended. If you have not had any experience attending a meeting, write the minutes for a historical event, such as the signing of the Declaration of Independence.

Writing Website Copy

You may need to write the text for a website, also known as the **copy**. The way a website is written is important for both the readers of the site and the search engines that find the page and deliver it in a search. Here are six guidelines for writing an effective website:

1. **Know your audience.** Much like giving a presentation (page 130), writing copy for a website requires knowing and understanding the potential readers. The intended audience should determine the style and tone of the copy. A corporate website for a manufacturer of pipes will have a totally different reader than a website for skateboarders.

2. **Write quality headlines.** Headlines grab the reader's attention and help focus them on a particular section of the website. Clear, concise headlines should capture the essence of what that section of the website is about.

3. **Be an expert.** Know your company's products and/or services and incorporate that knowledge into your copy.

4. **Engage your audience.** Use the active voice more than the passive voice. Depending on the type of company, product, or website, consider writing in a style that feels like you're having a conversation with the reader.

5. **Use key words wisely.** One purpose of copy is to attract search engines and provide the site with an online presence. The quality of your sentences and explanations on the topic will result in better search engine results than just a trail of key words.

6. **Solve a problem or fill a need.** Most people have a problem they're looking to solve. Your writing can show readers how your service or product is the perfect solution.

> **Now it's your turn to practice.**

Choose an object in your home or office. Write one or two paragraphs of website copy introducing that product and the company behind it, keeping in mind the preceding guidelines.

Awkward Mistakes to Avoid
Don't Press Send!

Especially in a business setting, poor word choice could reflect poorly on you. So, before hitting the Send button, look over your writing for these kinds of problems:

Colloquial or regional language:

This was *literally* the best day of my life.
I was, *like*, so surprised.

Double negatives (page 101)

Run-on or fragmented sentences:

Please don't leave any personal items in the conference room it is not courteous to your colleagues who are using the room after your meeting.
On the desk in the conference room where we had the meeting.

Use of slang, text abbreviations, or emojis

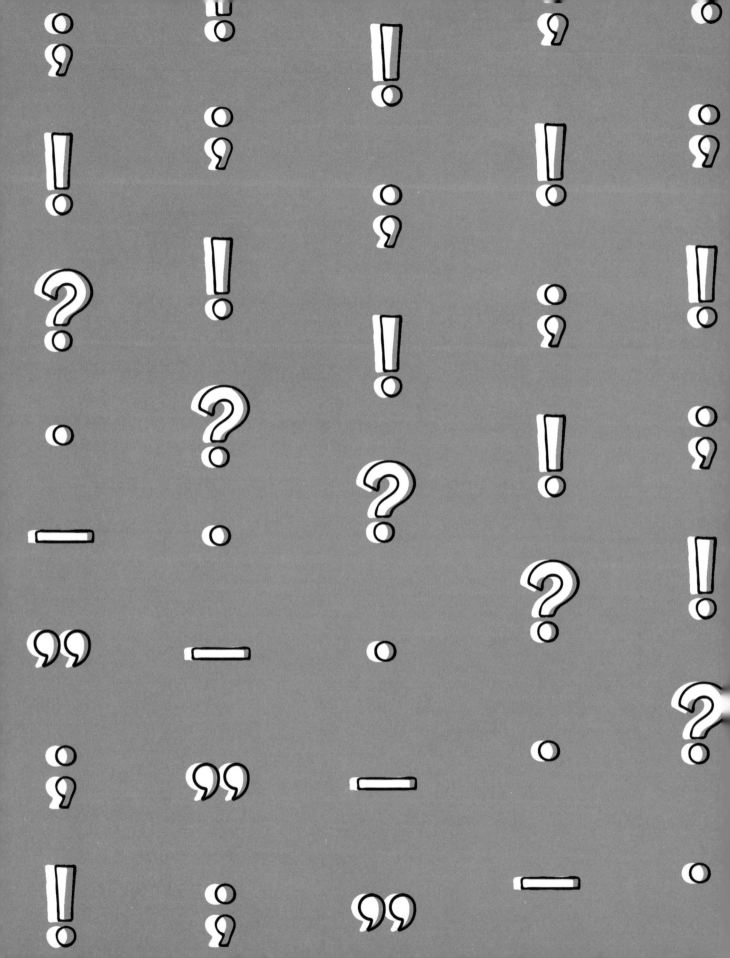

Chapter Thirteen

Social Situations

In this section, we will look at how to communicate appropriately and effectively in social situations. We'll start with invitations—how to write them and respond to them. We'll explore how to give thanks, send regrets, and even how to express your romantic feelings on paper. In addition, we will look at the language you can use in various situations, like finding a place to live, shopping, and seeking medical attention.

Event Invitations

Whether you're planning a formal event, like a wedding or business gala, or a child's birthday party, the invitation should be clearly written and informative.

Formal Invitations

For a formal event, start with the hosts of the party. Here are a few ways to open the invitation for a business event:

- You are cordially invited to attend the Acme Company Dinner Gala.
- The Acme Company invites you to the Dinner Gala.
- Please join the Acme Company for our 10th Annual Dinner Gala.

For a wedding invitation, the format may vary. Formal, traditional weddings list the bride's family first.

Mr. and Mrs. Adam West
Request the honor of your presence at the wedding of their daughter
Kay West
To
Denny Slate
Son of Mr. and Mrs. Larry Slate

After the introduction, write the date and time in words, not numbers.

Saturday, the Tenth of June
Two Thousand Twenty
At Five O'clock in the Evening

Lastly, include the name of the venue where the event will take place.

The Waldorf Astoria
301 Park Ave, New York City

Less formal events can contain more casual language.

Shhhhh! We're having a surprise birthday party for Tomoko!
Sunday, March 6, at 6:00 p.m.
Rosie's Trattoria, 35 Main Street, Harrison
RSVP Rosa at 212-555-1212 or rosaz@jmail.com

Using these tips, write an invitation to an event.

Casual Invitations

There are several different ways we can convey casual invitations in English.

Use **would you like to** followed by a base verb. **Would you like to** is a polite way to say **do you want to**.

1. **Would you like to** have dinner on Friday night?
2. **Would you like to** go to the park on Sunday?

In a similar way, we use **why don't we** followed by a base verb.

1. **Why don't we** go to a jazz club tomorrow?
2. **Why don't we** go for brunch on Sunday?

You can also use **I was wondering if** followed by a subject and verb.

1. **I was wondering if** you'd like to have dinner with me tomorrow night.
2. **I was wondering if** you'd be interested in seeing a play on Saturday.

When you know the person well, you can use **let's** followed by a base verb.

1. **Let's** go fishing next week.
2. **Let's** see if we can get tickets for the baseball game tonight.

Now it's your turn to practice.

Invite someone based on the prompt. Use the different invitation patterns shown on this page.

1. Invite a friend to a concert on Tuesday.
2. Invite a coworker to play billiards tonight.
3. Invite a romantic interest to dinner on Saturday.
4. Invite your neighbor to a barbecue.

Accepting Invitations

The language used to accept an invitation depends on the type of invitation received and the relationship with the person who sent the invitation. Formal and/or professional event invitations, like a job interview, meeting, or speaking engagement, typically require a formal response. The same applies to formal social events, like weddings, christenings, and bar/bat mitzvahs. Send your reply as soon as possible. Here are some examples of acceptance responses:

Job interview. Thank you very much for arranging an interview on Thursday, June 1, at 10:00 a.m. Our telephone meeting on Tuesday was very informative, and I look forward to meeting with you in person to discuss the position further.

Meeting proposal. Thank you for considering Acme Digital Services for your website project and for your offer to meet on Friday. I look forward to hearing your thoughts and presenting several ideas that we have in mind.

Speaking engagement. I am honored and delighted to have the opportunity to speak at your sales conference on September 4 at the Jarvis Center. I appreciate being chosen as one of the presenters.

Wedding invitation. Thank you for inviting me to share the joy with your family in celebration of the marriage of Isabel and her fiancé, Fabrizio. It will be my pleasure to join you on this special day.

When accepting a casual invitation, such as a verbal or text-message invitation, here are some phrases you can use. Including a *thank-you* or *thanks* is also appropriate.

1. Thanks. That sounds fun. I've never been to a jazz club before.
2. Thank you. That sounds nice.
3. I'd love to. Thanks so much.

Now it's your turn to practice.

Write a reply accepting an invitation in the following situations.

- You were invited to a friend's wedding.
- You've been invited to a face-to-face job interview after having a phone interview.
- Your YouTube channel is very successful, and you've been invited to speak at a media conference for college students.

Declining Invitations

The language you use to decline an invitation depends on the type of invitation you received and your relationship with the person who sent it. In general, declining an invitation should include both your regrets and a reason for declining, except for an invitation for a job interview. Here are some examples for graciously declining an invitation:

Job interview. When declining a job interview, it's not necessary to provide a reason, unless the reason is that you have accepted another position.

> Thank you very much for offering to meet me for an interview for the position. I regret to inform you that at this time, I have to decline the opportunity. I sincerely appreciate your time and consideration.

Meeting proposal. When declining a meeting proposal, offer an alternative when possible.

> Thank you for considering Acme Media for your upcoming project and your offer to meet this week. I'm afraid that our team will be unable to meet at this time. I anticipate being available at the end of April. Please let me know if that would be acceptable for your needs.

Speaking engagement. When declining an invitation to speak, suggest another person who may be able to do the job.

> Thank you for the invitation to speak at your sales conference on September 4. I regret to inform you that I have another commitment that week. You may wish to reach out to my colleague Brad Evans, who is a successful sales manager and engaging speaker.

Wedding invitation. When declining a wedding invitation, sending a gift is a thoughtful way to show that you care about the couple.

> Thank you for inviting me to share the joy with your daughter Isabel and her fiancé, Fabrizio. Regrettably, I will be away on business that weekend. I'm sorry I can't be there to celebrate with you.

Here are some phrases you can use to decline a casual invitation:

1. That sounds great, but I have other plans this weekend.
2. Thanks a lot, but I am going skiing on Friday.
3. Sounds great. Thanks, but I have a huge exam on Monday, and I need to spend the weekend studying.
4. I wish I could, but I've been invited to my cousin's graduation on Sunday.

Write a message to decline these invitations.

1. You were invited to a wedding of someone you are not very close with.
2. You've been invited to a job interview.
3. A classmate or coworker invited you to a beach party.
4. You have been invited to speak at a sales conference.

Thank-You Letters

After you've attended an event you were invited to, it's a good idea to thank the organizer or host. The language you use depends on the type of event and your relationship with the person who sent it. Here are different ways to express thanks.

Job Interview

After a job interview, send your thanks in an e-mail as soon as possible. It shows the interviewer your interest in the position as well as your integrity as a person.

> Dear Yelena, Thank you for taking the time to meet with me this afternoon. I gained a great deal of insight from our discussion, and I'm excited about the prospect of joining your team. I look forward to hearing from you.

Meetings

> Dear Kazu, Thank you and your team for meeting with me today. I feel the meeting was productive and insightful. I understand that you need to discuss our proposal with Mr. Zimper, after which time I look forward to the opportunity to move forward with our plans.

Speaking Engagements

> Dear Mr. Lusscroft, Thank you for inviting me to speak at your workshop. I enjoyed the positive energy in the room and the questions from your staff. I'd be happy to hear any feedback, and I look forward to speaking at a future event at Acme Media.

Weddings

Dear Franz and Gretchen, Thank you so much for the chance to celebrate Mina and Hank's special day. What a lovely affair it was. Clair and I had a wonderful time, and we wish the newlyweds a lifetime of happiness and joy.

After casual events, here are some of the phrases you can use to express your thanks:

1. Thanks a bunch for last night. I had a great time.
2. Thanks a lot for dinner yesterday. It was amazing.

> **Now it's your turn to practice.**

Write a thank-you message for the following situations.

1. Thank a friend who took you to Sunday brunch.
2. Send a thank-you to a recruiter who set up a job interview for you.
3. Thank the buyer who arranged a sales meeting for you.
4. Send thanks to the parents of the bride who invited you to a wedding.

Writing Love Letters

Anyone can go to the store on Valentine's Day and find a litany of preprinted greeting cards, but an actual, handwritten love letter becomes a cherished memory, like a photograph. It could be the letter you write inside a greeting card or a stand-alone letter. In either case, here's how you can write yours.

Start off with a greeting, like *My dearest Kate,* or *To my true love, Andrei.*

Next, explain why you're writing the letter: *As we celebrate our second Valentine's Day together, I wanted to share the strength of my feelings for you,* or *For our first anniversary together, I wanted you to know just how much you really mean to me.*

Then it's time to mention your feelings for them: *There's something special about your smile that makes my heart skip a beat.* You can then finish with some sentiment of your love: *I've never thought that my love for someone could grow as strong and as deep as it has for you.*

Lastly, end the letter by signing off with something special, like *Yours for eternity, Martín,* or *Forever yours, Joomin.*

If you have a special someone or significant other, try writing a love letter to them. Reflect deep within you to find words that express your unique feelings, and make it your own—resist the urge to quote a movie or song.

Finding Housing

Time for some housing vocabulary! In the United States, we refer to apartments in terms of the number of bedrooms. A **studio** has just one large room, usually with a small kitchen and a bathroom. A **one-bedroom apartment** is generally set up like a studio, but it also has a separate bedroom. Your choice of apartment may also be based on the amenities, or desirable features, such as washer/dryer, dishwasher, etc.

Most landlords will ask you to sign a **lease**, which is a contract between you and the landlord stipulating the terms and conditions of the deal. This deal will probably require you to pay a **deposit,** which is money that you give the landlord when you move in and that will be returned when you move out if there is no damage to the space. The lease also details the amount and due date of the rent and other items. The language of this contract will be formal.

When responding to a housing posting, take note of the information being asked for, like your name, your age, if you have any pets, and your available move-in date. First impressions are important, so be warm and friendly in your correspondence but professional, too—which means that contractions and casual vocabulary are okay but lack of proper punctuation and a respectful greeting and sign-off might be a misstep.

Now it's your turn to practice.

1. Imagine you're now looking to move to a new apartment. What are four things that are important to you (price, location, size, certain amenities, etc.)? Based on your answers, write a sample e-mail inquiring about the property.
2. Imagine you are the landlord of the place you live in now. Pretend it's for rent, and write a short description, including the size, amenities, price, location, etc.

Shopping

Let's look at some vocabulary and phrases that are helpful for shopping. Macy's was **having a sale** yesterday, so I went there after work. It seemed like almost everything was **on sale**. I found a nice sweater that I liked. It was **on sale,** too. Usually $125, it was **50% off**! I just had to have it! The **clerk** said that the sweater was a final sale, so I cannot return it. Final sale means the store won't give **refunds**, and you can't **exchange** or **return** what you buy, so choose carefully!

Let's look at the key vocabulary and phrases related to shopping.

1. Stores have a sale, or there is a sale at that store. A **sale** is a special event where items in the store have a cheaper price than usual.
   - Macy's is **having a sale** today.
   - **There is a sale** at the Gap today.

2. Items are on sale. This means the item has a cheaper price than usual.
   - I bought this dress **on sale**.
   - Everything is **on sale** on Black Friday.

3. To talk about a discounted price, we often use a percentage off, like **50% off**.
   - This sweater was **50% off** today.
   - I bought these shoes for **30% off**!

4. The person who works in a department store or clothing store is a **sales clerk**, or **clerk**. A **clerk** can help you shop and also works at the register. Supermarkets, grocery stores, and convenience stores have **cashiers**. A **cashier** works at the register only and doesn't help you shop.
   - The **clerk** in Macy's was very helpful.
   - The **cashiers** in that drug store are not so nice.

5. When you are not happy with what you bought, you may want to **return** it. **Return** means bring back to the store.
   - I want to **return** this sweater. It is too big.
   - Can I **return** this if my husband doesn't like it?

6. When you buy something and realize it is the wrong color or size, you may want to **exchange** it. **Exchange** means change something for something else.
   - I **exchanged** my sweater for a larger size.
   - Can I **exchange** this for a blue one?

7. When you **return** something, the store will **refund** your money. We use **refund** as a verb and a noun.
   - I would like to return this sweater. Is it possible to get a **refund**?
   - This is a final sale, so we cannot **refund** your money.

Now it's your turn to practice.

Fill in the blanks with the correct word or phrase.

1. Abercrombie is having _____ this week. a sale / on sale / for sale
2. Apple products, like the iPad, are never _____. a sale / on sale / for sale
3. Do you like my boots? They were _____ at Shoe World. a sale / 30% off / 50% on sale
4. The _____ at Macy's was very helpful. She found my size for me. cashier / clerk / staff
5. I wish there were more _____ at this grocery store. The lines are so long. cashiers / clerks / staffs
6. I can't _____ this blue T-shirt because I lost the receipt. return / refund / exchange
7. I will try to _____ this blue T-shirt for a red one. I hope they have one. return / refund / exchange
8. The clerk told me I need to have the receipt in order to get a _____. return / refund / exchange

Scheduling Medical Appointments

In the United States, we generally have a **family doctor** or **primary care doctor**. We visit this doctor in their private office. Sometimes this office is called a **clinic**. A **doctor's office** is usually an office with just one doctor and his staff. A **clinic** is typically a large office with several doctors. A **hospital** is a large building with many doctors and beds. You can stay overnight in a **hospital**, but not at a **clinic** or **doctor's office**. Depending on your insurance, you may need to visit your primary care doctor for a **referral** before visiting a **specialist** directly. A specialist is a doctor who specializes in something specific, such as a dermatologist (skin doctor), cardiologist (heart doctor), etc.

You go to the **doctor's office** or a **clinic** when it is not an emergency, like a cold, a rash, or a checkup. You go to a **hospital** for an emergency or for a procedure, like an operation.

You can say **go to the doctor** or **see the doctor.**

- I **went to the doctor** yesterday for a checkup.
- I had a bad cold, so I decided to **see the doctor**.
- I **went to the hospital** last week for surgery.

To go to the doctor's office or a clinic, you need to schedule **an appointment**. We usually **schedule a doctor's appointment** to **see the doctor**. Once we make the appointment, we **have an appointment**. Again, you can also say that you are going to see the doctor:

- I **made a doctor's appointment** for April 3.
- I **have a doctor's appointment** at three o'clock this afternoon.
- I'd like to **see the doctor** about pain in my back. When is she next available?

When you have an emergency, you **go to the emergency room** in a hospital. To go to the **emergency room**, you do not need **an appointment**. The **emergency room** is the place in the hospital where people with serious medical emergencies go in or are brought to by an ambulance.

- I **went to the emergency room** after I fell off the ladder.
- I feel dizzy. I think I should **go to the emergency room**.
- The ambulance **took Li Min to the emergency room**.

If the doctor in the emergency room thinks your condition is serious or you need additional treatment, you may **be admitted to the hospital**.

- I **was admitted to the hospital** for testing after the accident.
- **Assad is in the hospital** for an operation.

Choose the best answer based on the vocabulary presented on page 149.

1. Where would you go if you cut your finger badly while cooking?
   a) a clinic
   b) a hospital
   c) a doctor's office

2. Who would you most likely make an appointment to see if you caught the flu?
   a) a specialist
   b) your primary care doctor
   c) the doctor at a hospital

3. You need to make an appointment at this place.
   a) the hospital
   b) the emergency room
   c) the doctor's office

4. Which of these places probably has beds where you can stay overnight?
   a) the clinic
   b) the doctor's office
   c) the hospital

Discussing Medical Issues

Let's look at some vocabulary and phrases that you can use to talk about medical issues. Some grammar tips to keep in mind when describing what might be wrong or how you're feeling are the **have verb + a noun** (*I have a cold, she has a stomach-ache*) and the **feel verb + an adjective** (*I feel nauseous, she feels sick*).

Sick is an adjective, and we use **sick** with the **be** verb.

- **I'm sick**, so I'm going to stay home from work.
- Minh **is sick** today, so he's not going to school.
- Priya **was sick** all weekend, but she's better now.

Note: You can also say, "I became sick," "I got sick," or "I feel sick."

Cold, **bug**, or **virus** are nouns used to mean a sort of sickness. We use them with the verb **have**.

- I **have a cold**.
- Guilia **had a bug** last week, so she didn't go into work.
- Thom **had a virus** all weekend, but he's better now.

We also use the idiom *catch a bug*, which means to "become sick." When you say that you caught a bug, virus, or cold, it means that you're sick.

- I **caught a bug**, so I'm staying home from work.
- Juana **caught a virus** last week, so she didn't go to school.
- If you don't wash your hands, you might **catch a cold**.

We also use *have* to talk about medical conditions and symptoms.

- I **have** a runny nose. I **have** a headache. I **have** a sore throat. I **have** a cough.
- Kimlee **has** the flu.
- Mari found out she **has** high blood pressure.

In English, we use **take** for every kind of medicine: pills, tablets, and liquids.

- Yasmin **took** aspirin for her headache.
- I **take** vitamins every morning.
- The doctor said to **take** one dose of cough medicine twice a day.

Now it's your turn to practice.

Choose the best answer based on the vocabulary presented on pages 150 and 151.

1. I (am / caught / have) sick. I think I should go to the doctor.
2. Ian said he (has cold / is cold / has a cold) so he won't be in the office today.
3. I (am / caught / have) a bad headache. I'm going to leave work early.
4. The doctor told me to (have / take / drink) two tablets twice a day.

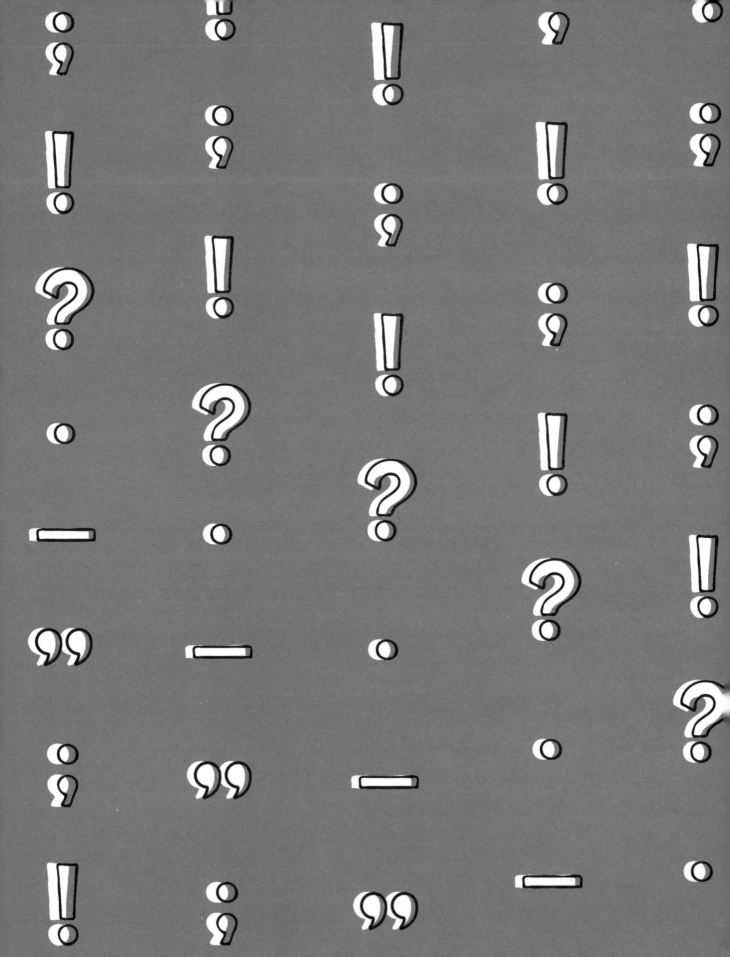

Chapter Fourteen

Getting Creative

Creative writing is a great way to hone your English skills in specific areas. Critical essays, for example, allow you to share your considered opinion with readers. You may be asked to write a critical essay in a college class or for even for a specialized blog. Practice with this kind of writing can lead into other areas, such as memoir, poetry, fiction writing, or even cultural criticism.

The Critical Essay

A critical essay is your interpretation of another work from film, literature, music, art, etc. In the critical essay, you introduce your reader to the work and present your analysis of it. If this is a school assignment, you may be asked to expand on a specific craft aspect or question about the work. For example, if you're reading "The Raven" by Edgar Allan Poe, your professor may ask you to analyze its use of symbolism, in which case your language and analysis must be formal, academic, and fully substantiated with evidence from the work itself. If you're writing a critical essay of a film for a website or blog, you might be able to focus on lighter themes instead and use language more accessible to an everyday reader as you review the work. Let's explore.

Introduction

In the introduction, you'll tell your readers the main idea of the work you are critiquing and then provide your **thesis statement**, which is the theory you're attempting to analyze and prove within the paper. For example:

> In *Diary of a Wimpy Kid*, author Jeff Kinney takes readers on an exploration of the trials and tribulations of life as a middle schooler. Through the author's use of naturalistic language, readers can more aptly feel the characters' emotions and make an authentic connection with the protagonist, Greg Heffley.

Summary

In the summary section, you'll discuss the details of the work in relation to your thesis, keeping it succinct and streamlined. For example:

> This novel is structured around the diary entries of Greg, a twelve-year-old boy who has just started middle school. As his story unfolds, readers are introduced to a number of impactful secondary characters, including his parents; his terroristic older brother, Rodrick; and his best friend, Rowley. The book begins with the first day of middle school and includes various moments from Greg's daily life and interactions with everyone around him.

Assessment and Analysis

In this section, you'll present your analysis of the work. In a critique, you might examine the good and not-so-good aspects of the work. For example:

> One major theme is Greg's desire to be more popular. The author does a thorough job of letting the reader know this desire from the very beginning of the book, where Greg mentions he is "around 52nd or 53rd most popular this year." (In a more analytical assessment, you'd revisit your thesis to provide the evidence necessary to prove it.)

Conclusion

The conclusion of the critical essay restates your thesis and summarizes the key points of the essay that help prove it.

> Through the perspective of Greg Heffley, the reader gets an in-depth look at life after elementary school. Greg tries hard to improve his popularity in his day-to-day dealings. While we never get to see how his rank changes, we are left reminded that life at this age is filled with unexpected challenges and emotions.

Now it's your turn to practice.

Write the introduction paragraph of a critical essay on the subject of your choice, setting up your thesis and illustrating how you intend to explore that topic. Keep the audience and context for the paper in mind when considering the appropriate language.

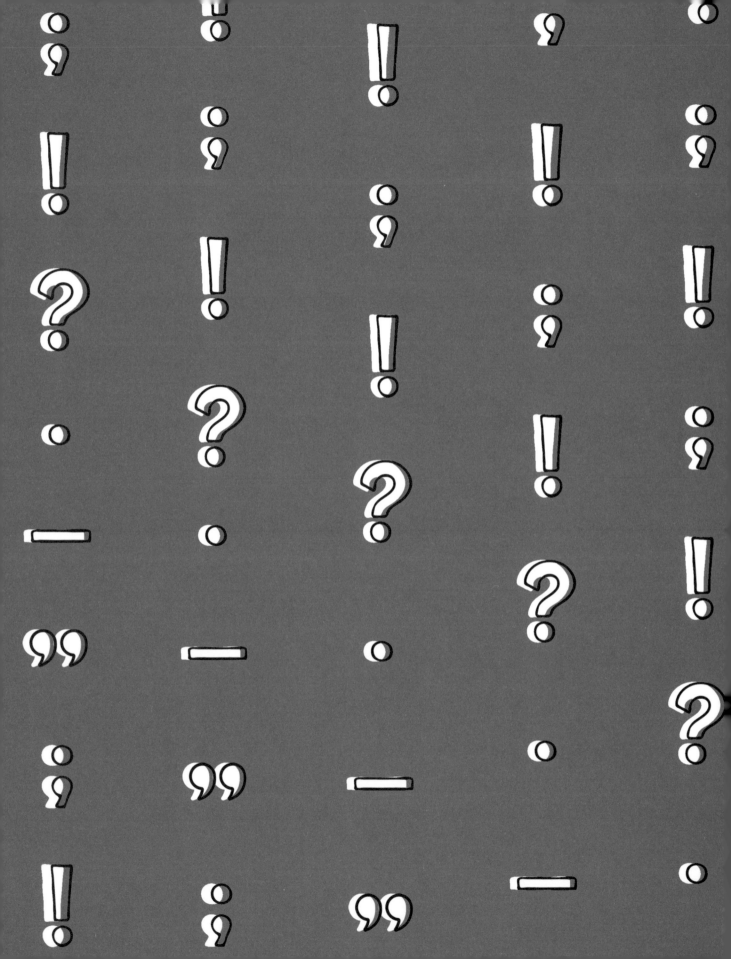

Chapter Fifteen

Our Digital World

Technology is constantly changing and at an increasingly fast pace. Historically, language has evolved along with new developments in technology, and it's important to understand this relationship. Language is always changing, and vocabulary and slang that people used even fifty years ago sounds archaic now. You'd have to watch an old black-and-white movie to hear people greet each other with *How do you do?* In this section, we'll look at this evolution of English, how text messaging has influenced our language, and how you can adapt to using English in the modern world.

Evolution of Technology and Language

Throughout history, new technologies have resulted in the creation of new and adapted language. Today, when you want to get some information about a topic, you **google** it. You **text** your sister and **e-mail** your customers at work, and then after work, you might **tweet** or **snap** your friends.

Technology also brings us new meanings by adapting old words. **Friend** is now a verb: You **friend** and **unfriend** people on social media. A **cloud** is a place for online data storage. A **cookie** went from a sweet baked snack to a piece of data on your computer. The noun **feed** may still be animal food on the farm, but in most places, it's the thread of information updated in your social media. A **tag** has gone from being a sticker on bread to a way to identify a person in a photo.

It's not just words that have been influenced by technology. According to a 2015 study by the Oxford University Press, the word **hashtag**, and its symbol, #, became a word that children under thirteen years old are using offline. First used to indicate relevant keywords on Twitter, "hashtag" came into popular use by people of all ages in everyday written language for "dramatic effect."

New ideas for words and grammar can even stem from memes, like "doing me a frighten," a meme in the voice of a startled dog in a type of "doggolingo" Internet language used in dog memes. Technically, the grammar of this sentence is incorrect—but in the language of a frightened dog friend, it's just right.

Lastly, it's hard to miss the text initialisms, or abbreviations, that have come into existence, such as LOL (laughing out loud), NVM (never mind), LMK (let me know), and IDK (I don't know). Language and grammar depend on the type of technology being used, but we can be certain that they will continue to change over time as technology and online communities evolve and influence one another.

Now it's your turn to practice.

Make a list of five new words or meanings for words (not discussed in this section) that have come into existence because of technology. Then use those words in a sentence, keeping in mind their new definitions and contexts.

Let's Talk about Texting

Text messaging, or **texting**, has had a tremendous impact on language. Texting is casual, conversational, and brief. In fact, texting is more like speaking than writing. That's because in many cases, people communicate via texting in real time, so what they type is usually similar to what they would say in person.

Texting and instant messaging have also increased the popularity of initialisms and emojis. Popular initialisms—acronyms like BRB (be right back), BTW (by the way), and OFC (of course)—made it quicker to express ourselves on cell phones of the pre-smartphone era, and symbols through typing came into favor to convey messages, such as :) for a smile, ;) for a wink, and :* for a kiss. As mobile communication became more advanced, little pictures, or emojis, replaced those symbols.

The language of texting is also generating its own brand of grammar. As noted in John McWhorter's 2013 TED Talk, LOL (laughing out loud) is being used in texting as a discourse marker, like **uh-huh**, **well**, and **you know**. For example:

> **Omar:** Do you wanna grab dinner after work?

> **Rick:** LOL I'm working until 10 p.m.

Rick isn't laughing about working until ten (although maybe he's laughing a sad, tired laugh at 9:30 p.m.). He's using LOL with the meaning of **ah**, **well**, or **no can do**. This type of usage of LOL has even made its way back into spoken English!

Now it's your turn to practice.

Write these initialisms and emoji sentences using English words.

CYL8R

LMK. TTYL.

🙏 for the ☕

The 🏔 here is 🔥

Adapting to Digital Communication

The advent of digital communication has provided both opportunities and challenges. Today, many people text and message more than they talk face-to-face or on the phone. Social media has introduced new ways of communicating with others through pictures, videos, and text. The digital world has provided the opportunity to socialize and work with others regardless of our physical locations, and this, too, has influenced how we use and think about language.

One area in which we still need to curb this modern communication style is in business situations. While short, ungrammatical phrases are perfectly acceptable in a text, they won't be well received in most business situations. This, of course, varies depending on the industry, but often, the language used is expected to be more traditionally, formally written—especially when communicating with clients. TY (thank you) is not appropriate to write when thanking a customer for a hundred-thousand-dollar order—in fact, it would be considered an insult. Generally, digital communication in the workplace is reserved for words, free of emojis and time-saving acronyms.

The ability to conduct business in a global environment means we're communicating with people in and from other parts of the world more than ever before. And while English is the international language of business, not everyone is fluent in nuances of the English language. Particularly when you are working in an international setting, self-awareness of the language you use can help you communicate more effectively. No matter the language you're speaking, try to avoid idioms and colloquial language your global colleagues may not understand.

A Final Word on Rule Breaking

Students and English learners often tell me they hear and see a lot of different kinds of English these days, and some of what they run into doesn't seem to follow a rule. They're right. In fact, there are a lot of times you actually don't need any of these rules when you communicate.

Mia: Hey!

Caden: What's up?

Mia: Hungry?

Caden: LOL totally

Mia: Pizza?

Caden: Awesome

Mia: Cool. Let's go

You may have conversations (verbal or text) like this all the time or know people who do. This brings us to context. Context—the setting you're in—is one of the most important concepts and guiding principles in any language. It's okay to bend or even break the rules, depending on the context. When applying for a job or asking a professor for an extension on a deadline, you'll follow the rules a lot more carefully than when responding to a casual invitation from your friend. In general, the more formal the situation, the more words and grammar you'll use. For example:

Thank you so much for studying here with me. I really appreciate it.
Thanks for studying here with me. I appreciate it.
Thanks for studying here. I appreciate it.
Thanks for studying.
Thanks a lot.

Keep Writing

As you come to the end of this book, you might ask, *What's next*? My advice: Write something every day. *But, Michael, what should I write?* Well, you can write in your diary, keep a journal, start a blog, or just use English more in your daily communication. The more you do it, the more you'll see your confidence and skills improving. This is your final assignment. Keep working at it, keep learning, and remember, your last mistake is your best teacher.

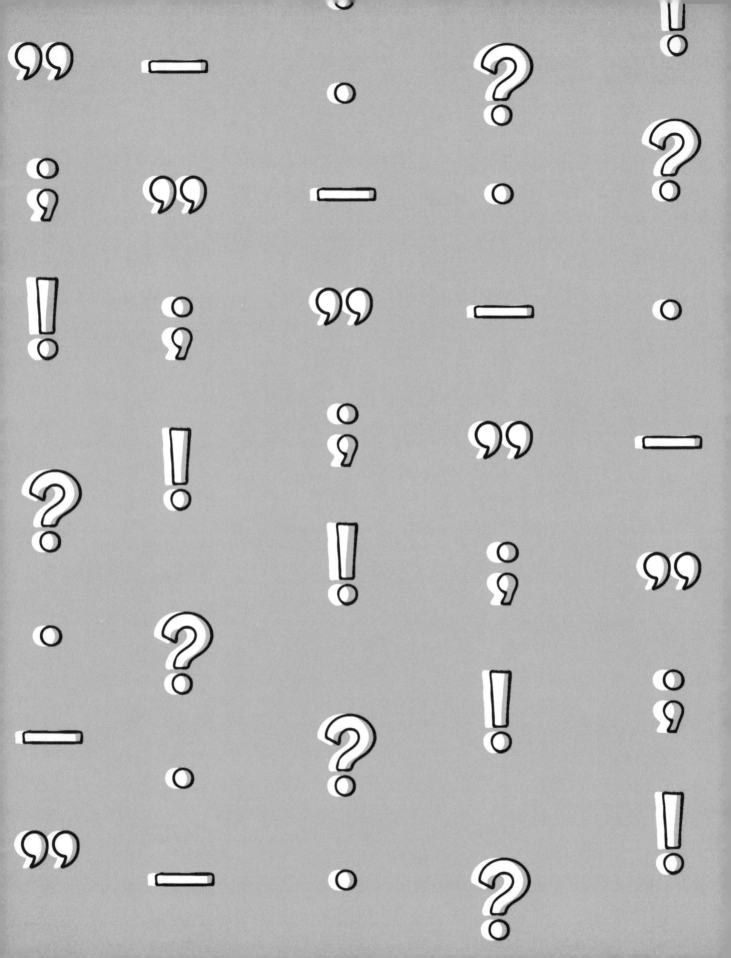

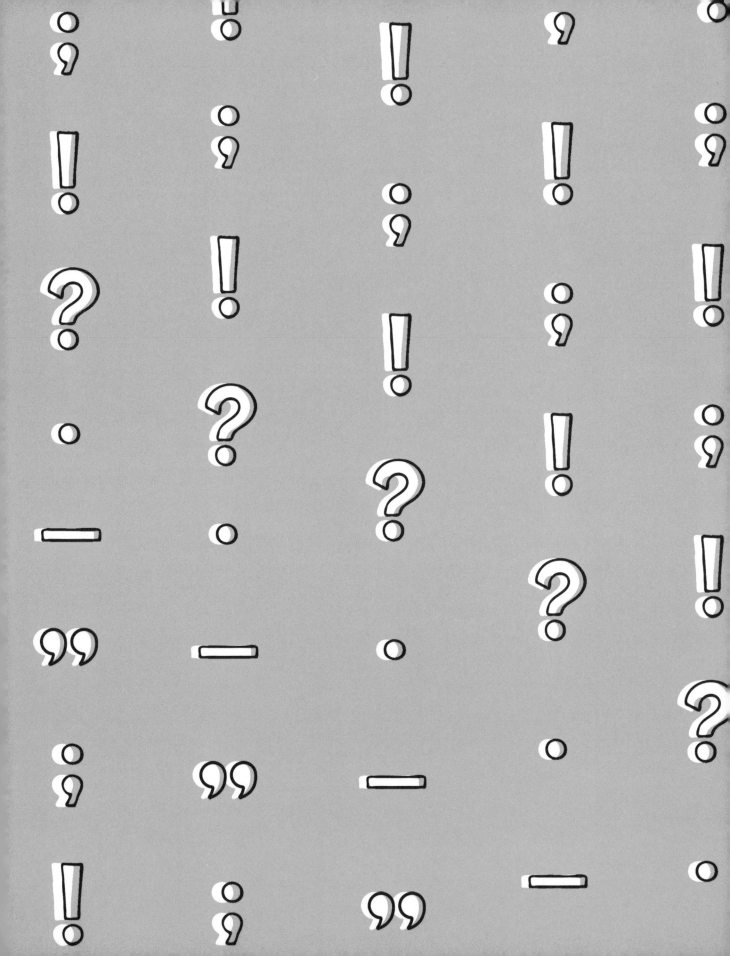

IRREGULAR VERBS CHEAT SHEET

Here are the present…past…past participle forms of the most common **irregular verbs**:

(Examples: Let's begin the meeting. The meeting began at 9:00 a.m. Don't enter the room after the meeting has begun.)

arise…arose…arisen
awake…awoke…awoken
be…was, were…been
bear…bore…borne
beat…beat…beaten
become…became
…become
begin…began…begun
bend…bent…bent
bet…bet…bet
bite…bit…bitten
bleed…bled…bled
blow…blew…blown
break…broke…broken
breed…bred…bred
bring…brought
…brought
build…built…built
burn…burned…burned
burst…burst…burst
buy…bought…bought
catch…caught…caught
choose…chose…chosen
cling…clung…clung
come…came…come
cost…cost…cost

creep…crept…crept
cut…cut…cut
deal…dealt…dealt
dig…dug…dug
do…did…done
draw…drew…drawn
drink…drank…drunk
drive…drove…driven
eat…ate…eaten
fall…fell…fallen
feed…fed…fed
feel…felt…felt
fight…fought…fought
find…found…found
fly…flew…flown
forbid…forbade
…forbidden
forget…forgot
…forgotten
forgive…forgave
…forgiven
freeze…froze…frozen
get…got…got
give…gave…given
go…went…gone
grind…ground…ground

grow…grew…grown
hang…hung…hung
have…had…had
hear…heard…heard
hide…hid…hidden
hit…hit…hit
hold…held…held
hurt…hurt…hurt
keep…kept…kept
kneel…knelt…knelt
know…knew…known
lay…laid…laid
lead…led…led
leave…left…left
lent…lent…lent
lie (recline)…lay…lain
lie…lied…lied
light…lit…lit
lose…lost…lost
make…made…made
mean…meant…meant
meet…met…met
overtake…overtook
…overtaken
pay…paid…paid
put…put…put

164

read…read…read

ride…rode…ridden

ring…rang…rung

rise…rose…risen

run…ran…run

say…said…said

see…saw…seen

sell…sold…sold

send…sent…sent

set…set…set

shake…shook…shaken

shed…shed…shed

shine…shone…shone

shoot…shot…shot

show…showed…shown

shrink…shrank…shrunk

shut…shut…shut

sing…sang…sung

sink…sank…sunk

sit…sat…sat

sleep…slept…slept

slide…slid…slid

smell…smelt…smelled

speak…spoke…spoken

spend…spent…spent

spread…spread…spread

stand…stood…stood

steal…stole…stolen

stick…stuck…stuck

sting…stung…stung

stink…stank…stunk

strike…struck…struck

swear…swore…sworn

sweep…swept…swept

swim…swam…swum

swing…swung…swung

take…took…taken

teach…taught…taught

tear…tore…torn

tell…told…told

think…thought
…thought

throw…threw…thrown

understand
…understood
…understood

wake…woke…woken

wear…wore…worn

win…won…won

wind…wound…wound

write…wrote…written

SPELLING CHEAT SHEET

Here are some words that are **commonly misspelled**:

1. a lot
2. accept (verb) / except (conjunction and preposition)
3. advice (noun) / advise (verb)
4. clothes (what you wear) / cloths (materials)
5. desert (dry, hot land) / dessert (sweet dessert)
6. effect (noun) / affect (verb)
7. every day (each day) / everyday (adjective)
8. its (possessive form of *it*) / it's (contracted form of *it is*)
9. lose (verb) / loose (adjective)
10. quite (adverb) / quiet (adjective)
11. their (possessive adjective) / they're (contracted form of *they are*) / there (adverb of place)
12. then (adverb) / than (conjunction and preposition)
13. your (possessive adjective) / you're (contracted form of *you are*)

Homonyms are two words that have the same spelling but different meanings.

1. address...(noun) location of a building / (verb) to give a speech
2. arm...(noun) part of a body / (verb) to give weapons or knowledge
3. back...(noun) part of a body / (verb) support
4. bat...(noun) an animal that can fly / (verb) to hit
5. book...(noun) an object you can read / (verb) to reserve
6. can...(noun) a container / (verb) ability
7. chip...(noun) a crispy fried snack / (verb) to break a small part
8. down...(noun) something made with feathers / (preposition) a direction
9. express...(adjective) quick or rapid / (verb) to say
10. fall...(noun) a season / (verb) to move down
11. fine...(noun) a monetary penalty / (verb) to charge money
12. foot...(noun) part of a body / (noun) a unit to measure length
13. grave...(noun) a resting place for the deceased / (adjective) very serious
14. hide...(noun) the skin of an animal / (verb) to conceal
15. junk...(noun) something worthless / (verb) to dispose of
16. kid...(noun) a child / (verb) to joke
17. park...(noun) an outside recreation place / (verb) to stop a car in a designated space
18. row...(noun) a line of seats, people, etc. / (verb) to paddle a small boat
19. sink...(noun) a wash basin / (verb) to collapse downward
20. trip...(noun) a short journey / (verb) to stumble

PARTS OF SPEECH CHEAT SHEET

These nine **parts of speech** are the building blocks of sentences. Knowing them will lower your likelihood of writing an incorrect sentence.

adjective	describes a noun or pronoun (lucky, cold, blooming, wary)	The *fluffy* kitten sought *comforting* attention from its *exhausted* owner.
adverb	modifies an adjective or verb by indicating how, when, or where (*slowly, today, south*)	My mom *clearly* described the event *yesterday* by *slowly* enumerating each part.
article	determines whether a noun is specific (*the*) or nonspecific (*a, an*)	Give me *an* apple so that I can add it to *the* stew with *the* chicken and *the* onions.
conjunction	connects words, phrases, or ideas logically (*and, but, because, or*)	We ate cake *and* ice cream *but* no chocolate sauce *or* whipped cream.
interjection	an exclamation that indicates emotion or urgency (*so, ouch, dude, wow*)	*Oh! Hey!* You forgot your essay.
noun	a person, place, thing, or idea (*goats, politician, joy, San Francisco*)	*Jim* sat on the *ground* with his *son* to examine *bugs* under the *rock*.

preposition	connects a noun or pronoun to other words (*from, in, above, to*)	Ellie gave the essay *to* me *after* I climbed *onto* the dais *with* my computer.
pronoun	a word that substitutes for a noun or noun phrase (*he, yours, they, her*)	*They* realized *their* mistake immediately when *their* professor narrowed *his* eyes.
verb	an action word in all its forms (*went, sigh, laugh, weep, crawl*)	I *finished* my essay, and then I *leaped* onto the bar and *celebrated*!

Here are all the parts of a sentence, indicated one by one:

She [pronoun] saw [verb] the [article] extent [noun] of [preposition] the [article] errors [noun] in [preposition] John's [noun] writing [noun], and [conjunction] immediately [adverb] chose [verb] not [negation] to [preposition] date [verb] him [pronoun]. Wow! [interjection]

GLOSSARY

Here are basic grammar terms and phrases used in this book. These are good to know when you need to explain something but don't know a particular word.

acronym: a word made up of the first letters of the name of an organization

active verbs: verbs that represent an action

active voice: a type of sentence that has a subject before the verb

adjective: a word that describes a noun and indicates its characteristics

adjective clause (also relative clause): a clause that begins with a relative pronoun

adverb: a word that modifies a verb, an adjective, and another adverb

adverb clause: a clause that begins with a conjunction

adverbs of completeness: words that indicate a degree of completeness

adverbs of definite frequency: words that indicate exactly how often something occurs

adverbs of indefinite frequency: words that indicate imprecisely how often something occurs

adverbs of manner: words that indicate how something happens

adverbs of place: words that indicate location or direction

adverbs of time: words that indicate how long or how often something occurs

appositive: a phrase that modifies a noun

articles: words that indicate whether a noun is specific or unspecific

attributive adjectives: words that describe the size, color, texture, etc., of a noun

auxiliary verb: a helping verb

base: an infinitive verb used without **to**

capitalization: the uppercase form of a letter

clause: a group of words including a subject and verb but that is not a complete thought

common nouns: nouns that indicate things and places

comparative form: the adjective form used in comparing two or more nouns

complex sentence: a sentence containing one independent clause and one or more dependent clauses

compound noun: a word formed by two consecutive nouns

compound sentence: a sentence connecting two independent clauses

compound word: a word composed of two or more words

conclusion: the summary or ending section of an essay, letter, etc.

conditional: a sentence beginning with *if* or *unless* that indicates a condition

conjunction: a word used to combine two sentences into one sentence

contrast words: words that indicate that two or more nouns are different

copy: the text portion of a website or advertisement

countable noun: a word that represents something that you can count

dangling modifiers: a word or phrase that is not adjacent to the word it is modifying

definite article: the word *the*, which introduces a specific noun

demonstrative pronoun: a pronoun that indicates a specific thing

dependent clause: a clause that provides extra information about the preceding noun

determiner: a word that comes before a noun and identifies which noun we are talking about

emphasis adverbs: adverbs that give added certainty to the word they modify

emphasis: to show special importance

example words: words that illustrate or represent something

first person: the use of the pronoun *I* in writing or speech

focus adverbs: adverbs that are used to draw attention to particular words or phrases

gerund: an *-ing* verb that is used as or functions as a noun

indefinite article: the words *a* or *an* that introduce a nonspecific noun

independent clause: a complete thought that includes a subject and verb

infinitive: a base verb preceded by the preposition *to*

intransitive verb: a verb that is not followed by a direct object

meeting minutes: the official, written record of a business meeting

misplaced phrases: phrases which are placed far from the word or phrase they are modifying

modal verb: an auxiliary verb that indicates necessity or possibility

modifier: a word or phrase that provides extra information about the word that comes after it

noun: a word that indicates a person, place, or thing

noun clause: a clause that begins with a question word

participle: a verb form, such as the *-ed* or *-ing* form

passive voice: a sentence that emphasizes the result of the action of the verb

past participle verb: the form of the verb which is preceded by the auxiliary verb **have**

plural noun: a noun that represents more than one thing

possessive: a noun or pronoun that indicates possession

possessive adjectives: words that come before a noun to indicate who or what owns that noun

possessive noun: the *'s* form of the noun to indicate ownership

predicative adjectives: adjectives that describe the subject of a sentence and which follow the verb

preposition: a word that comes before a noun and indicates direction, location, or time

prepositional phrase: a phrase containing a preposition followed by a determiner and a noun

probability adverbs: adverbs that indicate a degree of probability

pronoun: a word that substitutes for a noun

proper nouns: words that indicate the name of a particular person or place

punctuation: various marks used to clarify the meaning of a sentence

quantifier: a word or phrase that indicates the quantity of a noun

relative adverb: the words *when, where,* and *why,* which are used join clauses

relative pronoun: a word that precedes a dependent clause

singular noun: a noun that represents one thing

split infinitive: a situation in which a word, usually an adverb, is placed in the middle of an infinitive

stative verbs: verbs that represent a state of being

superlative adjectives: adjectives which indicate the highest degree of comparison

superlative form: the adjective form used to indicate the highest degree of comparison

third person: the use of the pronouns *he, she,* or *it* in writing or speech

topic sentence: another word for the thesis or main idea of a paragraph

transitive verb: a verb that can be followed by a direct object

uncountable noun: a word that represents an abstract idea or thing

verb: a word that indicates an action or a state of being

ANSWER KEY

1. Countable Nouns
Sample answers

1. In my town there are a lot of stores and restaurants. There are also two big parks. There's just one museum, but there is a small art gallery as well.
2. My kitchen has a lot of coffee cups and glasses. We have three apples, an orange, and two bananas. There are many appliances, including one coffee maker and one blender.

2. Special Plural Nouns
Sample answers

1. The boys wrote essays about spies, ponies, and toys while listening to waltzes.
2. The casinos in the cities have discos, where families take photos of spies sitting on couches.

3. Irregular Plural Nouns
1. *Incorrect: fish*
2. *Correct*
3. *Correct*
4. *Incorrect: people*
5. *Correct*

4. Uncountable Nouns

1.   U   C
   The beauty in this <u>wood</u> is shown in the <u>pattern</u>.

2.   U   U   C
   There is a lot of <u>garbage</u> and <u>junk</u> in the old <u>house</u>.

3.   U   C   U
   We get a lot of <u>mail</u>. Some is from our <u>customers</u>, but much of it is <u>junk</u>.

4.   U   C   C   C
   Viktor has a lot of <u>furniture</u>, including several <u>chairs</u>, <u>tables</u>, and <u>sofas</u> in

         C
   his <u>apartment</u>.

5.   U   U   U   C
   All of the <u>beer</u>, <u>wine</u>, and <u>soda</u> is in the <u>cooler</u>.

5. Nouns That Can Be Both Countable and Uncountable
Sample answers

1. *I have some free time tomorrow.*
2. *I've used that software many times.*
3. *There isn't enough space in my locker.*
4. *I would like to travel in space someday.*
5. *I had a lot of nice experiences working in sales.*
6. *You can gain experience by doing an internship.*

6. Compound Nouns
1. bus stop
2. coffee cup
3. living room
4. fire drill
5. tennis racket
6. warm-up
7. notebook
8. bookstore
9. dinner table

7. Hyphenated Nouns
1. It's a seven-day refund policy.
2. It was a three-day conference.
3. It's a twenty-pound box.

8. Capitalization
1. There is going to be a presentation on the first three presidents of the United States on Monday, January 3.
2. Bill Gates is the founder of Microsoft.
3. The Amazon River in South America is the second-longest river in the world.
4. We watched the Hollywood classic *Gone with the Wind* in my social studies class today.

9. Determiners

1. There is *a* man at *the* front desk in *the* lobby who can help Ø you.
2. I think we need to buy *a* new TV. *The* one in *the* living room is broken.
3. We met Jane's Ø husband and Ø son at *a* party last night.
4. My sister told me that Ø Franco's is the best French restaurant in *the* city.
5. Can you ask *the* boss if we can go Ø home early tomorrow?

10. Using *a* and *an*

1. We are staying at *a* hotel on the beach.
2. Sorry, but I really don't like Ø football.
3. I would rather listen to Ø music than watch *a* TV program.
4. Frida likes Ø art, so we went to *an* art gallery.

11. Using *the*

Sample answers

1. *I have a pet. The pet is a dog. The dog is white.*
2. *When I see the stars in the sky, I think of being an astronaut.*
3. *I prefer the kitchen. In that room, I really like my kitchen table because I can eat and do homework there.*
4. *I like jazz. The saxophone is a nice instrument, and I would love to have the chance to learn to play like Sonny Rollins.*
5. *My friends the Smiths like to go to the beach in the summertime. The Ismails like water sports and fishing. The Lis like art and often go to a museum.*

12. Possessive Adjectives

1. I can't find *a* pen, so can I borrow *your* pen or pencil?
2. I saw Daniela today. The stylist did a great job on *her* hair.
3. Diego had Ø shoulder pain because he got hit in *his* shoulder playing softball.

13. Demonstrative Pronouns

1. *Correct*
2. *Correct*
3. *Incorrect: that restaurant.*
4. *Incorrect: these employees*
5. *Incorrect: those girls*

14. Some and Any

1. Why don't you put *some* sugar or maple syrup on your oatmeal?
2. Do you have *any* time to have a meeting tomorrow?
3. Would you like *some* mustard or ketchup on your fries?
4. I need *some* hair wax. Do you have *any* ?
5. Here are the exam results. *Some* of you passed the exam, and *some* of you didn't. If you have *any* questions about your grades, come see me after class.

15. *Each* and *Every*

1. *Incorrect: every six months*
2. *Correct*
3. *Correct*
4. *Incorrect: each foot*
5. *Correct*

16. *Many, Much,* and *a Lot of*

1. Greg doesn't have *many* friends, even though he's lived here a year.
2. I don't think we have *much* time to visit that museum.
3. There was *a lot of* rain last month, and that's why we have so *many* flowers.
4. I think too *many* people don't realize how *much* effort it takes to run a business.
5. The rooms in this house have so *much* space.

17. *A Few* and *a Little*

1. *Correct*
2. *Incorrect: so little time*
3. *Correct*
4. *Incorrect: a little money*

18. Adjectives

Sample answer

Zhang Li decided to cook dinner. He bought an *ancient* cookbook that has *fabulous* recipes. When he saw a recipe for chicken soup, he thought to himself, *This looks* *tasty*. So he went to the store and got some nice *pink* carrots and a nice *triangular* onion. Then he went home and cooked the soup. He made a mistake with the time and ended up cooking the soup *30* hours longer than he should have. His family thought the soup was *super*.

19. Attributive and Predicative Adjectives

1. *Incorrect: something useful*
2. *Correct*
3. *Correct*
4. *Incorrect: a big suitcase*
5. *Incorrect: a child asleep on the sofa*

20. The Order of Adjectives

Part 1

Sample answers

Medical: medical exam, medical doctor, medical insurance, medical instrument
Portable: portable grill, portable fan, portable speaker, portable chair
Glass: glass door, glass plate, glass wall, glass cover

Part 2

Sample answer

I have a large, old, round, black, Japanese, iron, portable grill.

21. Adjective Comparisons

Sample answer

I have a toaster, a coffee maker, and a microwave oven. The toaster is smaller than the microwave oven. The microwave oven cooks faster than the toaster. The toaster is the oldest appliance in the room.

22. Participle Adjectives

Sample answers

1. The Museum of Modern Art is interesting because it has a variety of art.
2. Kyle is amazing because he can cook well, he's good at sports, and he's a funny guy.
3. I think a trip to Machu Picchu would be very exciting.
4. I was very bored at the last company meeting with our CEO.
5. I am very interested in learning more about world history.

23. Adverbs of Manner and Place

1. It was snowing hard last Sunday.
2. It's a nice day so let's go outside.
3. It's challenging to live and work abroad.
4. The children play together nicely.
5. I will call you when I get downtown.

24. Adverbs of Time

Sample answers

1. I go to the gym once a week.
2. I never work overtime.
3. Sometimes I go on a business trip.
4. I usually get to the office at 8:30 a.m.
5. I read the newspaper every day.

25. Other Types and Positions of Adverbs

Sample answers

1. I almost missed my train recently.
2. I also speak Japanese.
3. I hardly go bowling.
4. Venere is certainly the best restaurant in my town.

26. Active versus Stative Verbs

1. What (are you working / ~~do you work~~) on today?
2. I (have / ~~am having~~) a lot of things to bring to the conference.
3. Since everyone (~~is agreeing~~ / agrees) with the terms, let's sign the contract.
4. I (~~study~~ / am studying) hard because final exams start tomorrow.
5. This cookie (tastes / ~~is tasting~~) a bit too sweet.

27. Verbs Followed by Gerunds

Sample answers

1. In the office, I dislike using spreadsheets.
2. Last night I finished eating dinner at 7:00 p.m.
3. I'm exercising more and I think I will keep doing that.
4. My school prohibits smoking anywhere on campus.
5. I regret not studying hard enough last year.

28. Verbs Followed by Infinitives

Sample answers

1. I would advise my classmate to focus on studying instead of taking a job.
2. During meetings, I tend to speak up.
3. I would refuse to cheat on an exam because I am scared I would get caught.
4. I taught my coworker how to use a pivot table.
5. I've decided to visit the Grand Canyon for my next vacation.

29. Verbs Followed by Either Gerunds or Infinitives

1. *Incorrect: stopped to smoke*
2. *Correct*
3. *Incorrect: tried plugging it in*
4. *Correct*

30. The Three Forms of the Verb

1. I always (listen) to the radio in the car on the way to work.
2. I (went) to Stockholm in 2017.
3. They usually (spend) a lot of time in the office on the weekends.
4. We (bought) a new car last month.
5. Can you (help) me with my project?

31. Simple Present

1. We *need* to finish this project by Friday.
2. The professor *wants* us to work in groups.
3. I really *think* I have to cut down on drinking coffee.
4. She has a high GPA because she *studies* hard.
5. You *cook* very well. Did you learn from your grandmother?

32. Simple Past

1. I heard Emily *persuaded* the boss to let us go home early on Friday.
2. The only way we can improve profits is to *cut* costs.
3. The reason you *lost* points on the essay is that you forgot to write the conclusion.
4. The professor *organized* a field trip to ABC Labs.
5. Have you *identified* the problem with the e-mail server?

33. Simple Future

Sample answers

1. I am going to go to work tomorrow.
2. I'm going shopping on Saturday.
3. I think it will keep raining tomorrow.
4. Work starts at 8:30 in the morning.

34. Present Perfect

1. *Correct*
2. *Incorrect: We visited her*
3. *Correct*
4. *Incorrect: Nora was a student*
5. *Correct*

35. Past Perfect

Sample answers

1. I had studied English for four years before I got this book.
2. I had attended a language school before studying at this school.
3. I had studied the past perfect tense before getting this book.
4. I had always thought that.
5. In my last English class I studied idioms. I had not studied those idioms before.

36. Future Perfect

Sample answers

1. I will have finished a big project by noon tomorrow.
2. By next month, I will have started a new job.
3. By next year, I will have gotten my MBA.
4. By the time I am twenty-eight, I will have started medical school.
5. By the time I retire, I will have become a millionaire.

37. Present Progressive

1. *Correct*
2. *Correct*
3. *Correct*
4. *Incorrect: The sales meeting starts*
5. *Correct*

38. Past Progressive

Sample answers

1. I was eating breakfast thirty minutes ago.
2. I was working on a budget.
3. I was listening to some Mozart last night.
4. Five years ago, I was living in Miami.
5. I was close with my uncle. He was always telling us interesting stories.

39. Future Progressive

Sample answers

1. I will be eating lunch an hour from now.
2. I will be starting work tomorrow morning at 9:00 a.m.
3. I will be living in the same place in five years' time.
4. I think my boss will never be retiring.
5. I will be finishing studying the lessons in this book soon.

40. Present Perfect Progressive

Sample answers

1. There are reference books all over the table because I have been studying.
2. I have been taking notes for several hours.
3. I have been looking at those beakers for two hours.
4. The boss's door has been closed all day because he is hiring someone.
5. I have been working on an experiment in the lab all night.

41. Past Perfect Progressive

Sample answers

1. The accounting manager was fired because he had been stealing money from the company.
2. A guy walked into me on the sidewalk because he had been texting.
3. Madelyn passed all of her final exams because she had been studying very hard.
4. Isaac fell down at the holiday party because he had been dancing.
5. I was able to understand this lesson because I had been studying it very carefully.

42. Future Perfect Progressive

Sample answers

1. By this time tomorrow, I will have been working here for exactly one year.
2. By my next birthday, I will have been living in California for six months.
3. By this time next week, I will have been married ten years.
4. By the time I finish all of the lessons in this book, I will have been studying for two months straight.
5. By the time I retire, I will have been managing my own company.

43. Modals Part 1: *Must / Have to / Need to*

1. My flight is at 7:00 a.m. tomorrow, so I *need to* wake up at 4:00 a.m.
2. When you have a job interview, you *must not* be late.
3. Paisley is lucky. Even though she is the store manager, she *doesn't have to* work on weekends.
4. The boss said the marketing plan we submitted looked okay, so we *don't have to* make any changes.
5. I think I *need to* start looking for a new job. This company isn't doing well.

44. Modals Part 2: *Had Better / Should / Ought to*

1. The sales rep *should* be here soon. He is usually on time.
2. This meeting schedule looks fine to me, but I think we *had better* have Elena look it over before we send it out.
3. The doctor told David that he *had better* stop smoking.
4. I think you *had better* go back and make sure you locked the door.
5. I think I *ought* to should start exercising. I need to lose a little weight.

45. Modals Part 3: *May / Might / Can*

1. I haven't finished my work, so I *may / might* stay here a bit longer.
2. Why don't you ask Cameron to help you? He *can* use all of the software.
3. Nicolas is a nice guy, but sometimes he *can* talk forever.
4. Grace wasn't feeling well, so she *may / might* not come to work today.
5. Some questions on the TOEFL *can* be tricky, so read them carefully.

46. Modals Part 4: *Could*

Sample answers

1. I wasn't able to play tennis two years ago.
2. I was able to keep my GPA above 3.5 last semester.
3. I don't think it could snow within the next seven days.
4. I don't think an AI robot could replace me at work.
5. I think I could have studied harder over the past year.

47. Causatives

Sample answers

1. My boss makes me start work at 8:00 a.m.
2. If I were the boss, I would let my staff wear casual clothes to work.
3. My coworker had me help them with the spreadsheet this morning.
4. It would be impossible for anyone to get me to wake up at 5:00 a.m. to go hiking.
5. I want to have my house painted.

48. Conditionals

1. *Incorrect: water freezes*
2. *Correct*
3. *Incorrect: if I had known about it*
4. *Correct*
5. *Correct*

49. Prepositions of Time

1. The final exam begins *at* 4:00 p.m.
2. The next team meeting is *on* June 3.
3. The nursing course only starts *in* the spring semester.
4. I can't believe the boss is making us work *on* the weekend.
5. Charlotte became the office manager *in* 2002.
6. There's not much traffic *at* night.

50. Prepositions of Location

1. Aliyah met her husband when she was working *at* Yahoo.
2. I was *at* work until 11:00 p.m. trying to finish the marketing project.
3. I didn't realize you were *in* the kitchen.
4. Scarlett lives *on* the south side of the city.
5. The speaker system is *in* the middle of the table.

51. Preposition Collocations

Sample answers

1. Keeping up with changes in technology is necessary for success in the twenty-first century.
2. I've made an attempt at playing golf recently.
3. I participated in an HR seminar last week.
4. I am familiar with three foreign languages.
5. I was impressed by my manager's speech last month.

52. Phrasal Verbs

Sample answers:

ask out, back up, cut out, end up, find out, give up, kick out, look after, make up, put out, take in, turn off, etc.

53. Basic Sentence Structure and Clauses

1. *Independent clause*
2. *Dependent clause*
3. *Independent clause*
4. *Dependent clause*
5. *Dependent clause*

54. Compound and Complex Sentences

1. Even though Manuel had the necessary experience and qualifications, he was turned down for the job.
2. We recorded the CEO's speech, which he gave at the conference.
3. Carson wasn't able to pass the final exam because he didn't put enough effort into studying.
4. Yumi likes to study in the public library, which has a number of private study rooms.
5. We won't be able to start the meeting until everyone has arrived at the office.

55. Adjective Clauses, Noun Clauses, and Adverbial Clauses

Sample answers

1. I remember a time when there was no Internet.
2. Can you tell me where the conference room is?
3. Unless we work faster, we won't be able to finish this project.
4. The boss asked me to work this weekend, which doesn't make me very happy.
5. Technology, which affects all of our lives, advances at an incredible rate these days.

56. Commas, Hyphens, Dashes, and Apostrophes

The First Day on the Job

Today was the first day of work for the part-time and full-time trainees at Acme Corporation's headquarters in LA. Even though everyone's mood was upbeat and they were open-minded, many of them were a little on edge. One of the trainees' tasks was to read the company's HR handbook—the whole handbook! It's over thirty-five chapters. Actually, they were given ample time to complete the task, and some of the trainers were on standby to assist them.

57. Colons and Semicolons

1. Ana graduated from university in three and a half years; her next goal is to pass the CPA exam.
2. We need to set up the conference room with the equipment for the meeting: the projector, the remote control, and the screen.
3. There are three ways to grow your business: social media, which will attract potential customers; a mailing list to keep in touch with current customers; and a website to provide information about your business.
4. Many new managers face the same problem: They try to keep the same relationships that they had before becoming a manager.
5. I'll never forget what my grandfather used to tell me: Always keep your sense of humor and never worry about anything you can't control.

58. Parentheses and Brackets

1. Her research described the effects of Prohibition (1920–1933) on the New York City economy.
2. To enter the building, you need to (1) show a photo ID, (2) pass through the metal detector, and (3) pass through the facial recognition scanner.
3. The major automakers [Ford, GM, and Chrysler] use parts produced by a number of factories in Mexico.
4. The volume of work produced by Natsume Sōseki [one of the most famous figures in Japanese literature] rivals that of Franz Kafka.

59. Quotation Marks

"Have a seat, Mr. Jameson," said the lawyer. "This won't take long."

Mr. Jameson sat back on the sofa. He had a curious look on his face, and he could not understand why they were staring at him. He looked right at the lawyer's face and said: "Let's get to the point. What do you want me to do?"

"It's important for us to find the truth. A man's life is at stake," replied the lawyer.

Their eyes met. "I think the truth is clear, don't you?" Mr. Jameson asked.

"What exactly," chimed the lawyer, "is clear? We want to hear that from you."

60. Active and Passive Voice

1. The report was completed by Eli.
2. (no passive sentence possible)
3. The student advisor solved the issue.
4. (no active sentence possible)
5. (no active sentence possible)

61. Double Negatives

1. *Correct*
2. *Incorrect: he never travels*
3. *Correct*
4. *Incorrect: I seldom have*
5. *Incorrect: I haven't done anything*

62. First and Third Person

Sample answers

I thought *The Godfather* was a well-made drama. In addition to getting a look at the activities of an organized crime group, we could see how important family life was to the characters . . .

The Godfather was an acclaimed dramatic film. In addition to presenting the activities of an organized crime group, this movie provides a glimpse into the importance of family life for the characters . . .

63. Wordiness

Sample answer

Even though company policy contains rules regarding employee attendance, many employees arrive late. The company president has asked me to inform everyone that if you are late more than three times, you may face termination.

64. Misplaced Words and Sentence Logic

Sample answers

1. When I walked away from the counter, the coffee cup fell on the floor.
2. He was talking quickly, which confused me.
3. Wash your hands often to prevent colds.
4. I think only my sister knows my mom's recipes.
5. I read in the company newsletter that the CEO is going to give a speech.

65. Topic Sentence

Sample answers

1. People enjoy the rush of adrenaline from participating in extreme sports.
2. I cannot support the plan to build a new shopping mall in my neighborhood.
3. I prefer to work at home rather than at the office.

66. Paragraph Body

Sample answer

The greatest invention of the twentieth century was the computer. First of all, the computer allows people to work more efficiently and accurately. Its software can be used for word processing, complex calculations, and the creation of presentations. In addition, computer databases help workers record and extract information significantly faster than manual systems. Furthermore, computers make it possible for people to work together even if they are in distant physical locations.

67. Paragraph Conclusion

Sample answer

Such workplace enhancements are only possible with computers.

68. Transition Words

Sample answer

Technology has given us more options for communication. First of all, mobile phones allow people to communicate with others regardless of their physical location. For instance, text messaging provides a way to instantly contact a friend or family member. Additionally, social media gives us the opportunity to reach a wide group of people at one time, and platforms such as YouTube make it easy for anyone to broadcast their ideas and opinions to a global audience. As a result of the development of these different options for communication, people can keep in touch with others in ways that were not even imaginable in previous generations.

FURTHER READING AND RESOURCES

My website, myhappyenglish.com, contains additional free English lessons, tips, and tricks, covering phrasal verbs, idioms, and so much more English that you may often hear but not know what it means. It also features the Happy English Podcast with weekly English lessons.

Here are some additional favorite books and websites where you can continue building your English knowledge and find answers to more complex grammar questions.

Books

The Blue Book of Grammar and Punctuation, Jane Straus

Complete English Grammar Rules, Farlex International

The Elements of Style, William Strunk, Jr.

English Grammar (Series), Betty S. Azar

ESL Grammar, Mary Ellen Muñoz Page

Grammar in Use (Series), Raymond Murphy

A Manual for Writers of Research Papers, Theses, and Dissertations, Kate L. Turabian

Oxford Modern English Grammar, Bas Aarts

Perfect English Grammar, Grant Barrett

Practical English Usage, Michael Swan

Websites

English Club: englishclub.com/grammar

English Grammar: englishgrammar.org

English Grammar Online: ego4u.com

Grammar Girl: Quick and Dirty Tips: quickanddirtytips.com/grammar-girl

Grammarly Blog: grammarly.com/blog/category/handbook

Guide to Grammar and Writing: guidetogrammar.org/grammar/index.htm

Learn American English Online: learnamericanenglishonline.com

Learn English British Council: learnenglish.britishcouncil.org/english-grammar-reference

Perfect English Grammar: perfect-english-grammar.com

Purdue Online Writing Lab: owl.english.purdue.edu/owl

REFERENCES

Brown, Mark. "Hashtag Named UK Children's Word of the Year #Important." *The Guardian*. May 27, 2015. https://www.theguardian.com/technology/2015/may/28/hashtag-named-uk-childrens-word-of-the-year-important.

Buruma, Ian. "The Sensualist." *The New Yorker*. July 13, 2015. https://www.newyorker.com/magazine/2015/07/20/the-sensualist-books-buruma.

Kinney, Jeff. *Diary of a Wimpy Kid*. New York: Amulet Books, 2007.

McWhorter, John. "Txting Is Killing Language. JK!!!" Filmed February 2013 in Long Beach, CA. TED video, 13:36. https://www.ted.com/talks/john_mcwhorter_txtng_is_killing_language_jk.

Merriam Webster's Collegiate Dictionary, 11th ed., Springfield: Merriam-Webster, 2014.

The Official Guide to the TOEFL Test, 3rd ed. New York: McGraw-Hill, 2009.

INDEX

ABOUT THE AUTHOR

 **Michael DiGiacomo** started teaching English as a foreign language to adults at a private language school in Sendai, Japan, in 1994. In 2010, he formed Happy English, his own ESL tutoring company in New York. He teaches private lessons, hosts a podcast, and has a YouTube channel to help students all over the world learn English.